Origami
for the Connoisseur

by Kunihiko Kasahara
and
Toshie Takahama

Japan Publications, Inc.

Published by JAPAN PUBLICATIONS, INC., Tokyo and New York

Distributors:
UNITED STATES: *Kodansha International/USA, Ltd., through Farrar, Straus & Giroux,
19 Union Square West, New York 10003.* CANADA: *Fitzhenry & Whiteside Ltd., 195
Allstate Parkway, Markham, Ontario, L3R 4T8.* BRITISH ISLES AND EUROPEAN
CONTINENT: *Premier Book Marketing Ltd., 1 Gower Street, London WC1E 6HA.*
AUSTRALIA AND NEW ZEALAND: *Bookwise International, 54 Crittenden Road, Findon,
South Australia 5007.* THE FAR EAST AND JAPAN: *Japan Publications Trading Co., Ltd.,
1–2–1, Sarugaku-cho, Chiyoda-ku, Tokyo 101.*

First edition: March 1987
Fourth printing: January 1991

LCCC No. 86–80218
ISBN 0–87040–670–1

Printed in Japan

Foreword

Many years have gone by since I founded the New York Origami Center, an unprecedented institution at the time. Today, the center can be said to have fulfilled richly its initial goal of presenting Origami to a wide general audience. Origami fans are now surprisingly numerous, and considerable number of outstanding researchers in the field have emerged to elevate the quality of Origami dramatically.

It is true that a large number of books on the topic have appeared, but most of them are introductions for beginners. Certainly books of this kind are effective in carrying Origami to a wider audience. But, observing the degree of popularity it has already attained, for the sake of continued development, I have long wished for a book that would offer readers and devotees explanations of the very latest advances in Origami. That is why I wholeheartedly applaud the appearance of this book, which is precisely what I have been hoping for.

Perhaps a little difficult for the beginner, this book should nonetheless stimulate the reader's sense of adventure and spirit of challenge to the world of the unknown. Even after successfully duplicating the folds on the basis of the clear, thoroughly well-explained figures, the reader will find that a perusal of the accompanying explanatory texts reveals delightfully novel approaches and new Origami possibilities.

Today numbers of Origami fans are constantly increasing in many countries of the world. Consequently, the appearance of a thought-and-idea-filled book of this kind in English—a language understood by many different peoples—is a source of great joy. It is my hope that Origami devotees who are already in the forefront of the field will use this book to continue their study and advance to still greater heights.

Lillian Oppenheimer

Preface

A limitless universe of possibilities is concealed in the small—usually about six inches to a side—square of paper used in folding origami. The forms hidden, yet glimpsable, there range from those of vigorous animals to those of intellectually stimulating geometric figures. This book introduces the outstanding and delightful results of efforts of a group of people enthusiastically dedicated to journeying as far as they can into the universe of possibilities inherent in the square.

In the past, such people have apparently been divided into two categories: those in search of lyrical forms and those seeking geometric principles. As the reader will clearly see, however, in this book these two parallel paths have converged in one broad highway. For instance, the brilliant and totally original iso-area folding method of Toshikazu Kawasaki is outstanding in itself; but its great worth becomes all the more readily apparent when it is put to use in a variety of actual origami works. Such other recent discoveries as ways to fold paper to trisect discretionary angles and ways to arrive at cube roots $\sqrt[3]{2}$ by folding are certain to find application in many wonderful origami masterpieces.

This book has been compiled in the hope of stimulating the maximum number of people to participate in the search for the exhilarating world of limitless possibilities and fascinating thought waiting in the small square of paper six inches to a side. Of course, care must be taken not to be overwhelmed by the mountain of discarded paper this investigation inevitably entails.

Contents

CHAPTER 2:   CREASES HAVE MESSAGES TO MAKE   93

Symbols and Folding Techniques

----------	Valley fold
—··—··—··—·	Mountain fold
⟶	Move paper in this direction.
⟶	Fold behind.
⟹	Pull out. Open out.
⟹	Enlarge.
⟿	Pleat.
↻	Turn the model over.
⟵	Fold and unfold to make a crease.
＞	Sink. Push in.
⟹	Spread the layers and squash
	Inside reverse fold
	Outside reverse fold
	Completed
··········	X-ray view
⇨	Continued to next page.

Chapter 1

The Beauty and Delight of Geometric Forms

Logical and Lyrical

A geometric element can certainly be seen in origami, in which square forms are folded as accurately and carefully as possible. Indeed the famous German educator and founder of the kindergarten system Friedrich Froebel (1782–1852) thought highly of origami as a way of familiarizing children with geometric forms.

Once I, like many devotees, reacted unfavorably to hearing origami described in terms of geometry and mathematical principles. This is because *regular pentagon* and *cube* are words lacking the ability to inspire enthusiasm for creative ingenuity. I now realize, however, that this attitude is mistaken. To the best of my knowledge, more than fifty works can be devised on the theme of the cube; and each of them has its own individuality and appeal.

But, in many instances, origami consists in merely folding paper to discover possibilities; whereas geometric figures must be generated on the basis of principles. My former rejection of geometric and mathematic explanations of it was a preconceived notion based on the belief that origami belongs solely to the world of lyricism and is therefore totally different from cold theories.

Captious texts, like this one, however, will not get the point across. Since outstanding examples are far more convincing than all the verbal explanations in the world, as the reader enjoys the wide variety of different folds in this book, origami as a splendid fusion of both the logical and the lyrical should become much more apparent than any further words of mine could make it.

Making Froebel's Square

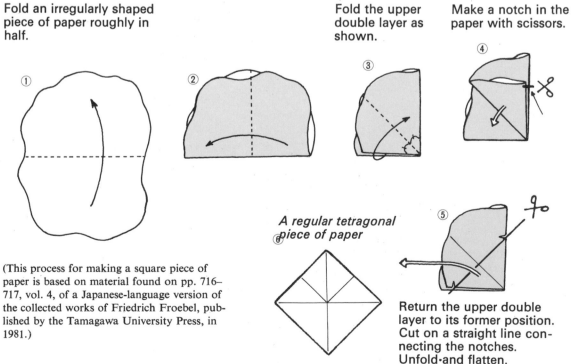

Fold an irregularly shaped piece of paper roughly in half.

Fold the upper double layer as shown.

Make a notch in the paper with scissors.

A regular tetragonal piece of paper

Return the upper double layer to its former position. Cut on a straight line connecting the notches. Unfold and flatten.

(This process for making a square piece of paper is based on material found on pp. 716–717, vol. 4, of a Japanese-language version of the collected works of Friedrich Froebel, published by the Tamagawa University Press, in 1981.)

Hourglass

Jun Maekawa

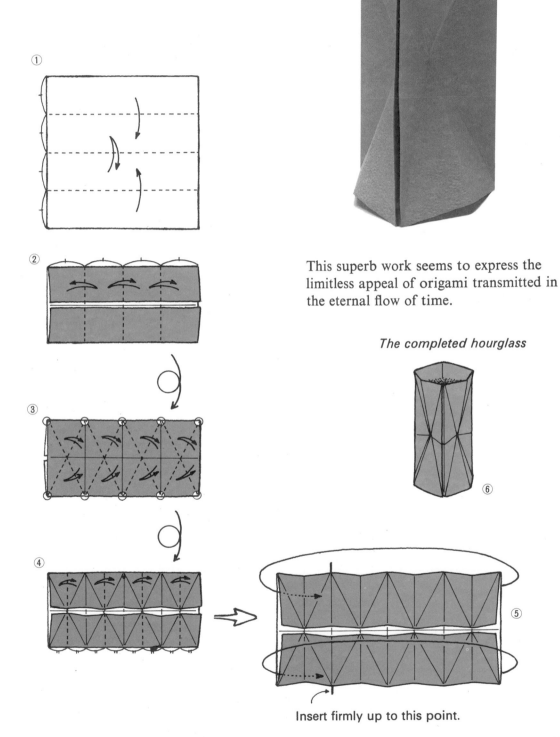

This superb work seems to express the limitless appeal of origami transmitted in the eternal flow of time.

The completed hourglass

⑥

Insert firmly up to this point.

Rotating Tetrahedron

Tomoko Fusè

Made with three sheets of paper, though it resembles the hourglass in folding and assembly method, this work has an interest all its own.

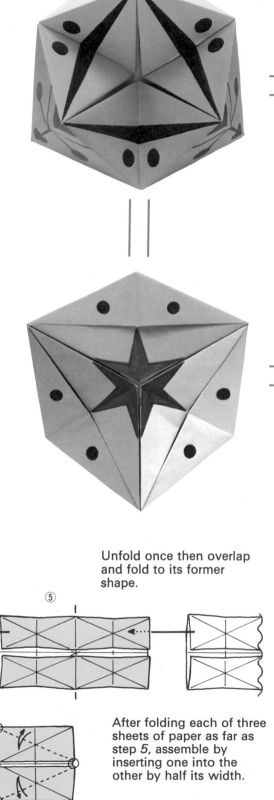

①

②

③

④

⑤

Unfold once then overlap and fold to its former shape.

After folding each of three sheets of paper as far as step *5,* assemble by inserting one into the other by half its width.

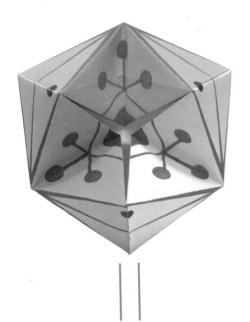

Origami Ideal

Although there is a tendency to regard those works produced by folding only one square sheet of paper, without resort to cutting, pasting, and drawing, as superior, such is the ideal for one but not all branches of the art. This work, which proves my statement, would be difficult and unattractive if produced within these narrow limitations. Something that is simple and duplicatable too is another origami ideal.

Completed fold

When the fold is at this stage, rotate several times to reinforce the creases.

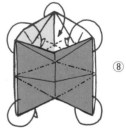

⑨

The fold is made more attractive by decorations of clearly different patterns like the ones shown in the photographs.

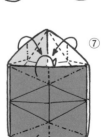

⑧

⑥

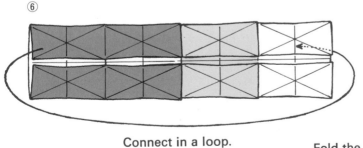

Connect in a loop.

Fold the creases inward.

⑦

The Meaning of Dividing

Some people claim that the method of teaching arithmetic in primary school, where addition and subtraction are presented before multiplication and division, is a mistake. They base their claim on the need to make use of actual experience. In home life, in parceling out treats with brothers and friends, children come into contact with division ahead of all the other arithmetic processes.

No matter whether this theory is well-founded, in origami carefully folding to align edges and corners amounts to making division of lines and angles into two, four, six, eight, and so on even parts. Divisions into such uneven quantities as three, five, and seven equal parts necessitate application of mathematical principles. Recent research into this problem has produced enough entertaining results to fill a separate volume. Here I present only a few interesting examples.

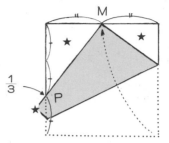

The Haga Theorem
Kazuo Haga

M = midpoint

1) The sides of the 3 right triangles formed at the star marks have length proportions of 3: 4: 5. The figures are therefore mathematically similar.
2) Point *P* demarcates one-third the length of the side.

Tsurifune

(Large folded crane suspended from a chain of several small folded cranes)

(From a classic called *Sembazuru Orikata* [Folding thousand-crane talismans], published in 1797.)

Paper needed to fold a Tsurifune

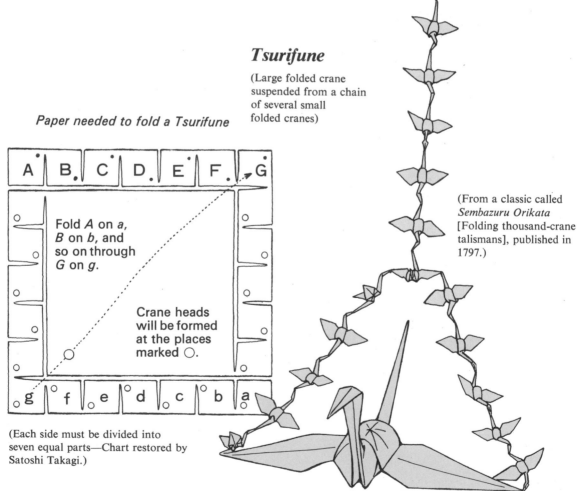

Fold *A* on *a*, *B* on *b*, and so on through *G* on *g*.

Crane heads will be formed at the places marked ○.

(Each side must be divided into seven equal parts—Chart restored by Satoshi Takagi.)

Expansion of the Haga Theorem

Kohji and Mitsue Fushimi

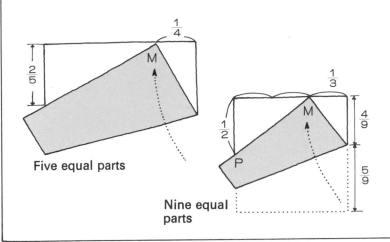

Five equal parts

Nine equal parts

This expansion of the Haga theorem involves repositioning the midpoint *M* on a side of a sheet of paper.

Brain Ticklers

The charm of this fold (quoted from the book entitled *Origami no Kikagaku* [The geometry of origami], published by the Nihon Hyōron-sha) is valuable for the pleasant exercise it affords the brain. I had a very good time working out proof for the one-fifth in *A*. Try your hand at it too.

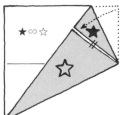

Author's Hint
From step *3*, make use of the similarity between right triangles ★ and ☆.

①
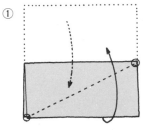

Fold only the uppermost layer.

②
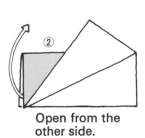

Open from the other side.

③
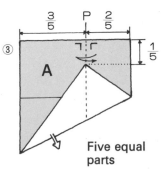

Five equal parts

④
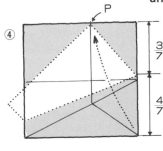

Seven equal parts

Lidded Cube Box

David Brill

This splendid box makes use of the way of making divisions into five equal parts shown in the preceding pages but is very difficult to produce.

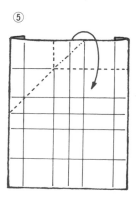

Division into five equal parts

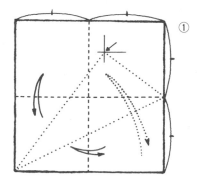

For steps *1* and *2*, it is a good idea to review instructions for divisions into five equal parts on the preceding page.

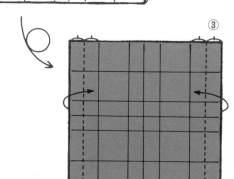

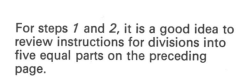

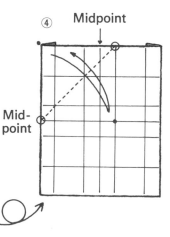

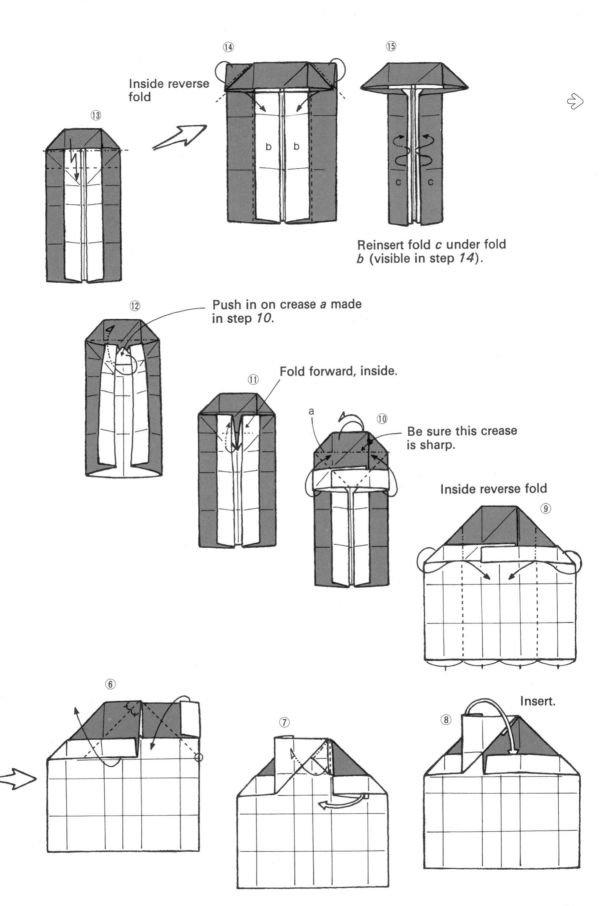

⑭ Inside reverse fold

⑮

b b

c c

Reinsert fold *c* under fold *b* (visible in step *14*).

⑬

⑫ Push in on crease *a* made in step *10*.

⑪ Fold forward, inside.

a ⑩ Be sure this crease is sharp.

Inside reverse fold

⑨

⑥

⑦

⑧ Insert.

21

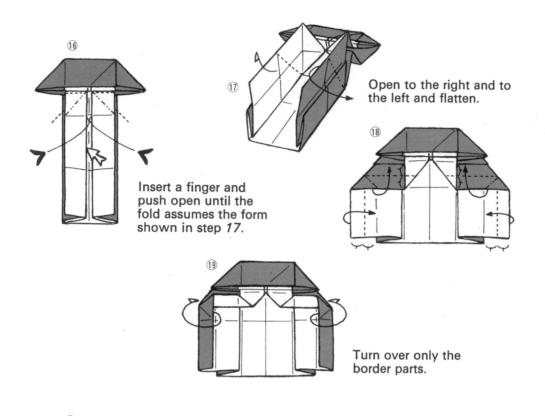

Insert a finger and
push open until the
fold assumes the form
shown in step *17*.

Open to the right and to
the left and flatten.

Turn over only the
border parts.

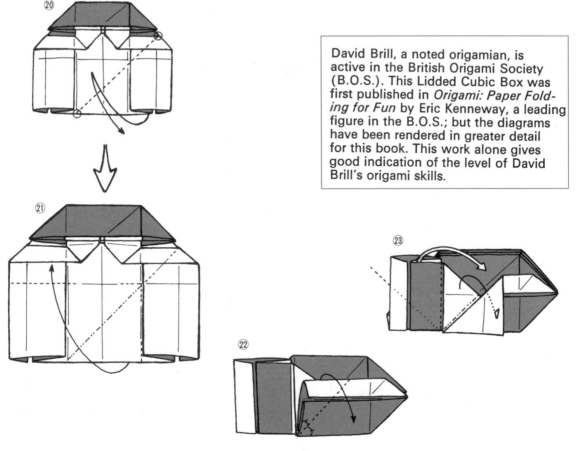

David Brill, a noted origamian, is
active in the British Origami Society
(B.O.S.). This Lidded Cubic Box was
first published in *Origami: Paper Folding for Fun* by Eric Kenneway, a leading
figure in the B.O.S.; but the diagrams
have been rendered in greater detail
for this book. This work alone gives
good indication of the level of David
Brill's origami skills.

Make all necessary adjustments
in the shape and put the lid on.

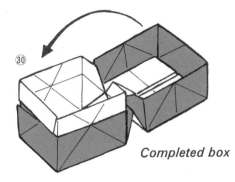

③⓪

Completed box

Once you have mastered the
method, fold again, without
making excess creases.

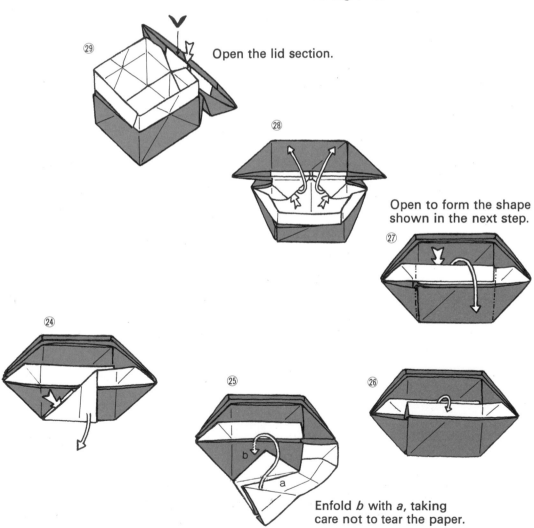

㉙ Open the lid section.

㉘

Open to form the shape
shown in the next step.

㉗

㉔

㉕

㉖

Enfold *b* with *a*, taking
care not to tear the paper.

Creases and Development Plans

As most fans already know, the appearance of Jun Maekawa on the scene has made the world of origami more fun than it used to be and has had an especially clarifying influence on basic forms and development drawings of folding lines.

For instance, an examination of the completed fold and of the development drawing on the right for his Extraterrestrial Being makes both the design and the unusual nature of the work readily understandable. People who find it difficult to proceed unless the process is clearly outlined can duplicate the development plan.

Toshikazu Kawasaki's system for folding to produce identical obverse and reverse surfaces on the following pages proves, however, that origami is endlessly fascinating and amusing because it goes beyond purely mechanical endeavors.

Before proceeding to that stage, I should like to make use of the following four folds to demonstrate how a simple change in folding order can work startling changes. If it were not for the difference between valley and mountain folds, charts *A*, *B*, *C*, and *D* below would look identical. This will be explained later, but now an examination of the finished cubes on the facing page will show how great a difference changes in mountain and valley folds and in folding order can make.

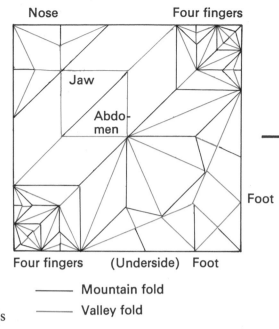

——— Mountain fold
——— Valley fold

Developmental Plan of Extraterrestrial Being

Various Unit Development Charts (all undersides)

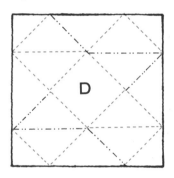

Tomoko Unit
(Double Joint)

Sonobè Unit

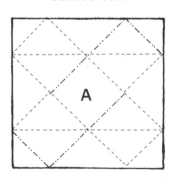

Simplified Sonobè Unit

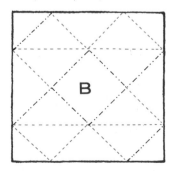

Bicolor *Ryugo* Unit

(In English-language works, what is called *unit origami* in Japanese is often referred to as *module origami*.)

Extraterrestrial Being

Jun Maekawa

Illustrated only with the development chart, the folding method looks like a sophisticated puzzle.

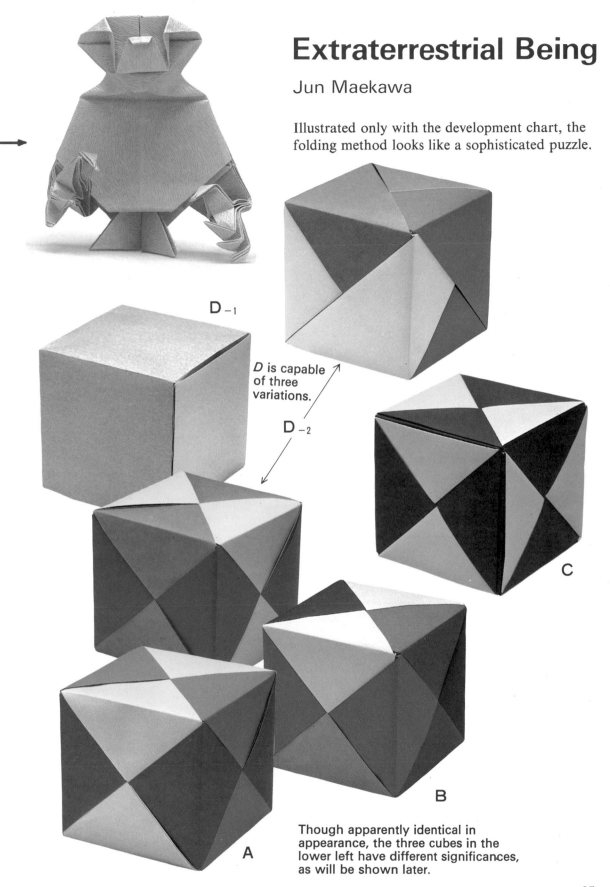

D −1

D is capable of three variations.

D −2

C

B

A

Though apparently identical in appearance, the three cubes in the lower left have different significances, as will be shown later.

Folding for Identical Obverse and Reverse Surfaces

Ordinary origami paper has color on one side (the obverse) and is white on the other side (the reverse). Most origami folds are designed to reveal the colored and conceal the white side. The Panda (*A*), however, makes more extensive use of the reverse white side than of the obverse black one. In the Malay Tapir (*B*), on the other hand, obverse and reverse are revealed to about equal extents.

But this is not what is meant by "folding for identical obverse and reverse surfaces." Equalizing the obverse and the reverse is achieved by the remarkable object called the Moebius strip, a band of paper or similar substance joined to form a loop in such a way that the obverse of one tip overlaps with the reverse of the other, producing something in which both are one. Applying a similar principle, Toshikazu Kawasaki developed his iso-area fold, shown in plane form in *D* and in solid form in *E*.

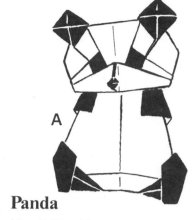

Panda
Kunihiko Kasahara

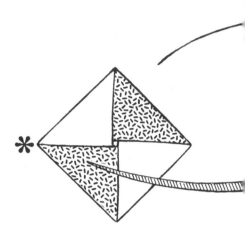

Iso-area (Obverse/Reverse) Folding Example I—Coaster #1

Toshikazu Kawasaki

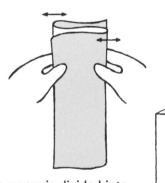

The paper is divided into three equal parts as shown above (this is the best way).

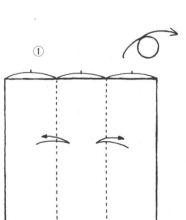

①

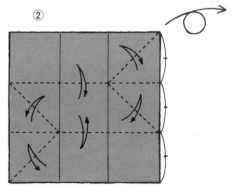

②

Comparing this fold with the traditional *menko* makes clear the significance of iso-area folding.

B **Malay Tapir** (p. 114)
Jun Maekawa

C **Moebius Strip**

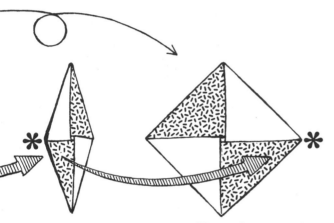

Since obverse and reverse are identical, this form is different from the traditional *menko*.

D

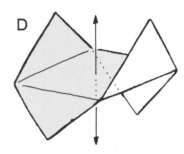

Principle of Iso-area Folding

E

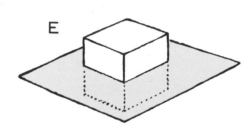

In Solid Form (pp. 30 and 34)

In the *menko*, obverse and reverse are different.

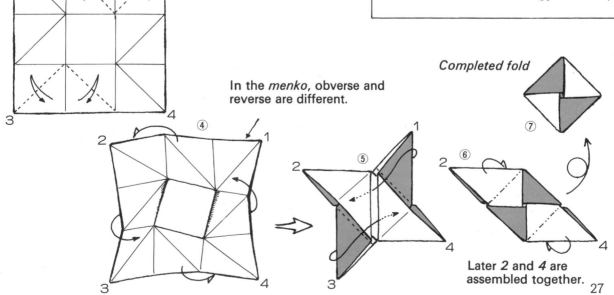

Completed fold

Later *2* and *4* are assembled together.

27

Iso-area Folding Example II—Coaster #2

Toshikazu Kawasaki

More technically advanced than Coaster #1, this work is training for making the following solid forms. The highly unusual folding methods in steps *4* through *8* were invented by Kawasaki himself. Master them now since the method occurs frequently hereafter.

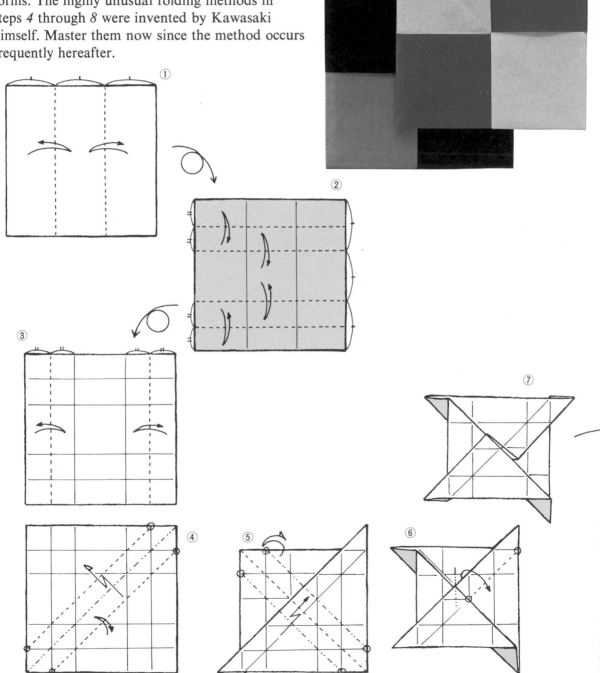

The Kawasaki Theorem of Creasing

When several creases are employed to fold paper into several layers, the sum of alternate angles around a pinnacle formed by those folds will equal 180 degrees or 2 right angles.

Explanation: This theorem means that the sum of alternate angles formed by fold lines from l_1 to l_8 in the diagram will equal 180 degrees. That is $a_1+a_2+a_3+a_4=b_1+b_2+b_3+b_4=180$ degrees.

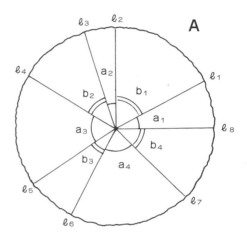

In addition to this theorem, Jun Maekawa has formulated another to the following effect: the difference between the number of mountain and valley folds used to fold a piece of paper flat into one surface is two. It is interesting to reflect on the relation between the two theorems.

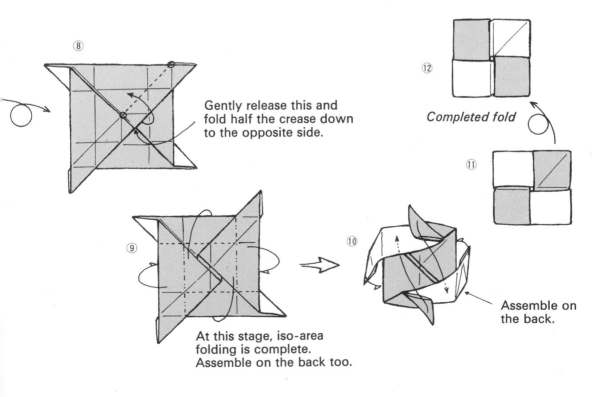

⑧ Gently release this and fold half the crease down to the opposite side.

⑨ At this stage, iso-area folding is complete. Assemble on the back too.

⑩ Assemble on the back.

⑪

⑫ Completed fold

Iso-area Folding Example III — Kawasaki Cube #1

Toshikazu Kawasaki

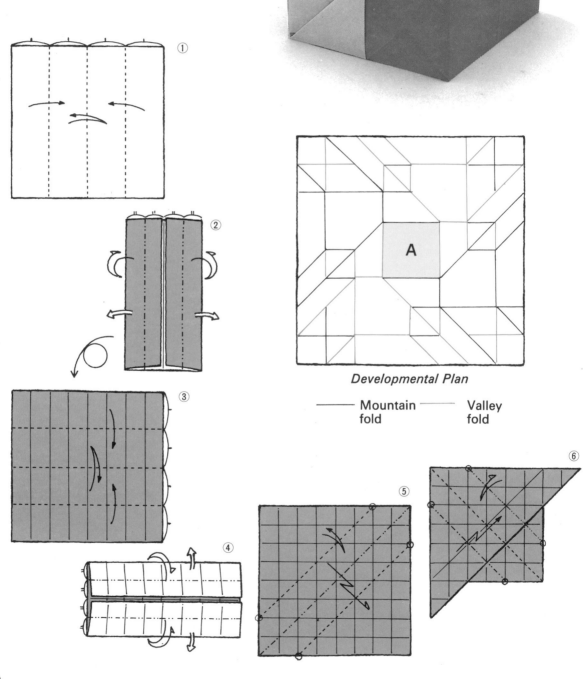

Developmental Plan

——— Mountain fold ——— Valley fold

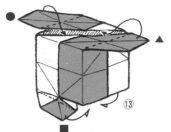

Although some people may be confused by the process between steps *10* and *11*, actually making the cube should clarify the meaning of iso-area folding. The principle behind new origami of this kind sounds difficult when explained verbally but becomes obvious when you do the folding. The examples on the next few pages will help you master both the theory and practice of this folding method.

Insert the flaps on the upper and lower sides as shown by the arrows.

From top to bottom, four places are always folded identically.

The center of the piece of paper, the part marked *A* on the developmental plan, is here.

Closely observing the positions marked ●, ▲, and ■, adjust to make a solid form.

The area marked ★ must be perpendicular to the square plane *A*.

Loosen and detach this.

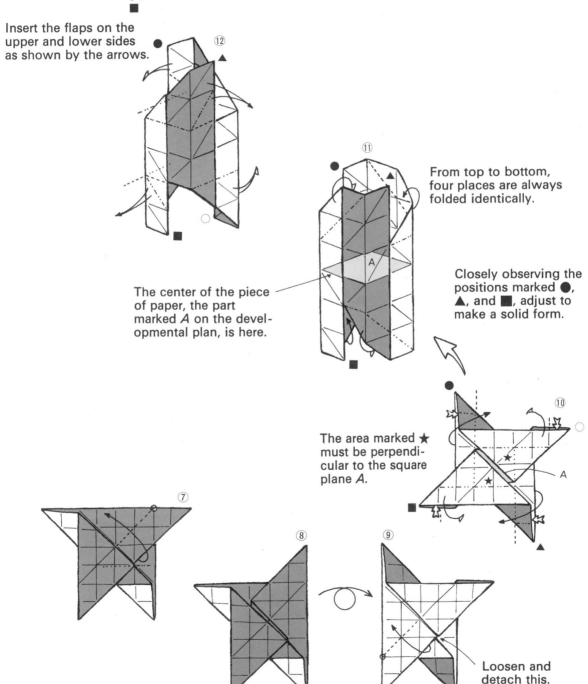

Variations of Kawasaki Cube #1

Toshikazu Kawasaki

Variation 1

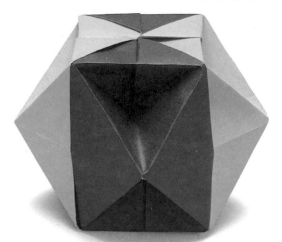

From a point midway the process of producing the cube on the preceding page, two interesting variations are possible. Aside from their significance as geometric-forms, they are introduced here as entertaining examples of origami. But, since the process diagrams are difficult to understand, it is better to work from the photograph and to regard the two as puzzles to be solved.

As diagram *A* shows, the first variation has eight of the corners of the cube inverted. (The red lines in the diagram are folding lines.) Keeping the idea of iso-area folding in mind and using the process charts below as hints, duplicate the form in the photograph.

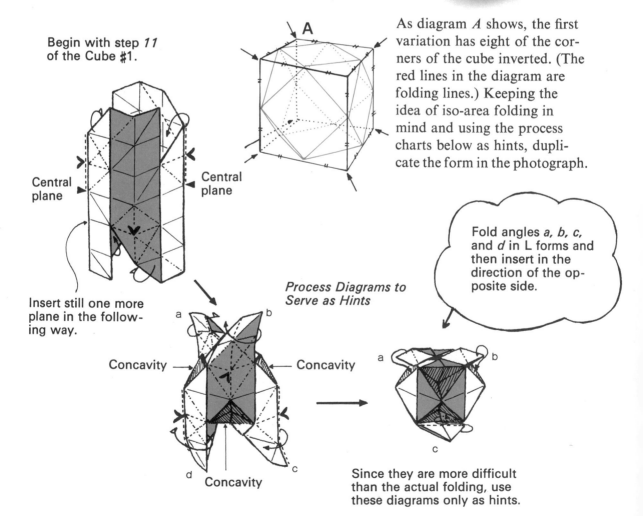

Begin with step *11* of the Cube #1.

Central plane

Central plane

Insert still one more plane in the following way.

Process Diagrams to Serve as Hints

Fold angles *a, b, c,* and *d* in L forms and then insert in the direction of the opposite side.

Concavity — Concavity

Concavity

Since they are more difficult than the actual folding, use these diagrams only as hints.

Variation 2

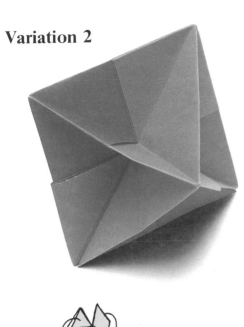

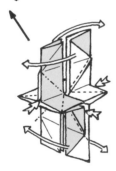

Insert the tips into the central gap, and the form is complete.

The central planes are firmly pressed into squares. The four beltlike sections are made to intersect with each other.

Process Diagrams to Serve as Hints

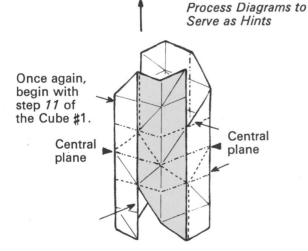

Once again, begin with step *11* of the Cube #1.

Central plane

Central plane

Cube and Octahedron

Although much less generally familiar than the cube (a regular six-faced solid figure), the octahedron (a regular, eight-faced solid figure) is nonetheless very lovely. Indeed Variation 2 of the Kawasaki cube represents the skeleton of the octahedron. A close examination reveals that this variation is composed of three intersecting square planes. Studying figures *B* and *C* below should make the nature of the octahedron clear.

Incidentally, the figure inscribed in red lines within the cube in figure *A* on the facing page, is a cuboctahedron, a basic solid-geometric figure about which more will be said later.

Regular octahedron and its framework structure

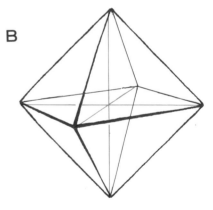

B

Relations between the cube and the regular octahedron

C

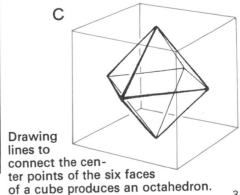

Drawing lines to connect the center points of the six faces of a cube produces an octahedron.

Iso-area Folding Example IV— Kawasaki Cube #2

Toshikazu Kawasaki

To ascertain the degree to which you have mastered this totally new, iso-area folding method, here is another solid figure produced by means of it. The folding method is more rhythmical and smooth in this than in the preceding instances.

Begin with step *11* of the Cube #1.

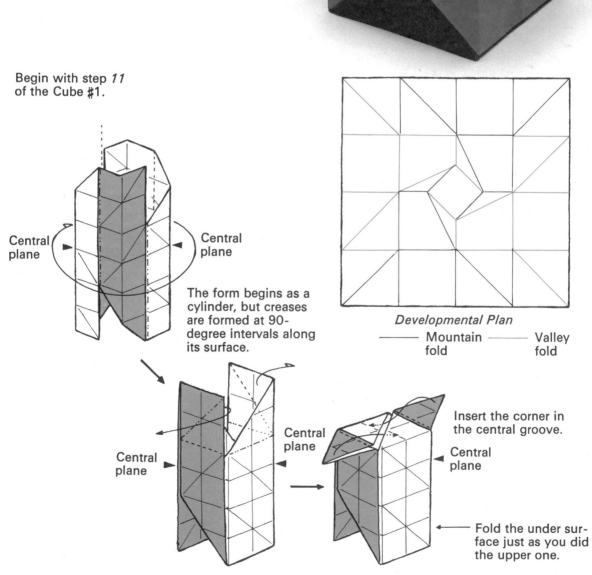

Central plane

Central plane

The form begins as a cylinder, but creases are formed at 90-degree intervals along its surface.

Developmental Plan

——— Mountain fold   ——— Valley fold

Central plane

Central plane

Central plane

Central plane

Insert the corner in the central groove.

Fold the under surface just as you did the upper one.

34

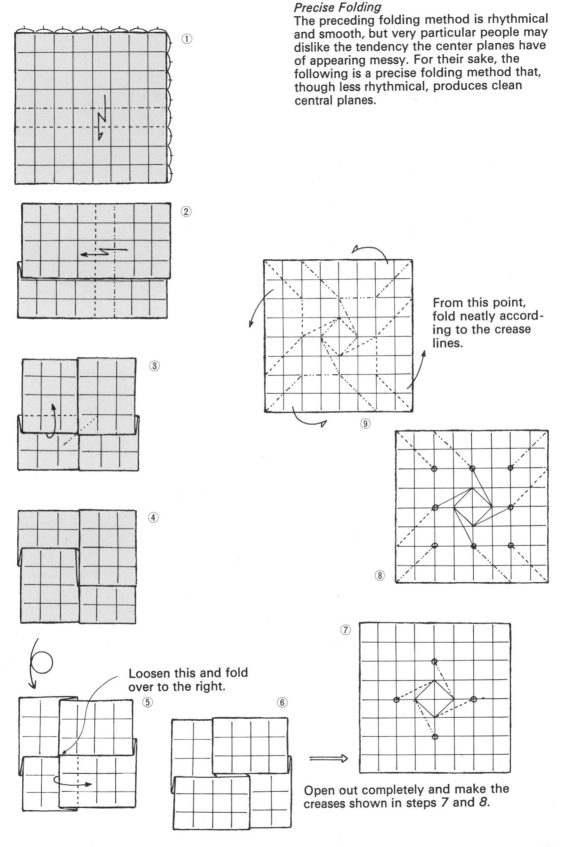

① ② ③ ④ ⑤ ⑥ ⑦ ⑧ ⑨

Precise Folding
The preceding folding method is rhythmical and smooth, but very particular people may dislike the tendency the center planes have of appearing messy. For their sake, the following is a precise folding method that, though less rhythmical, produces clean central planes.

From this point, fold neatly according to the crease lines.

Loosen this and fold over to the right.

Open out completely and make the creases shown in steps *7* and *8*.

Supersonic Reconnaissance SR-71

Toshikazu Kawasaki

This is one of the famous stealth planes that are untrackable by radar.

It is time to rest from purely geometric forms and have some fun. The iso-area folding technique is used in steps *9–11*.

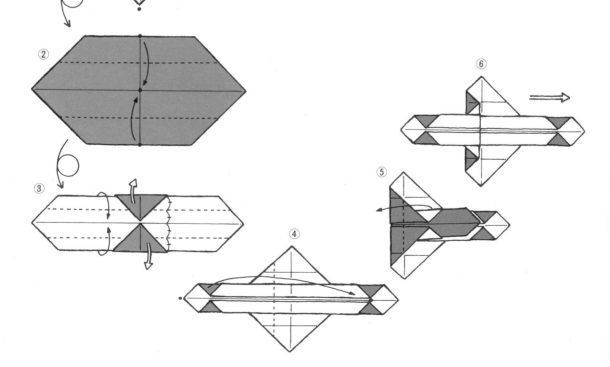

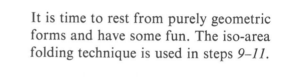

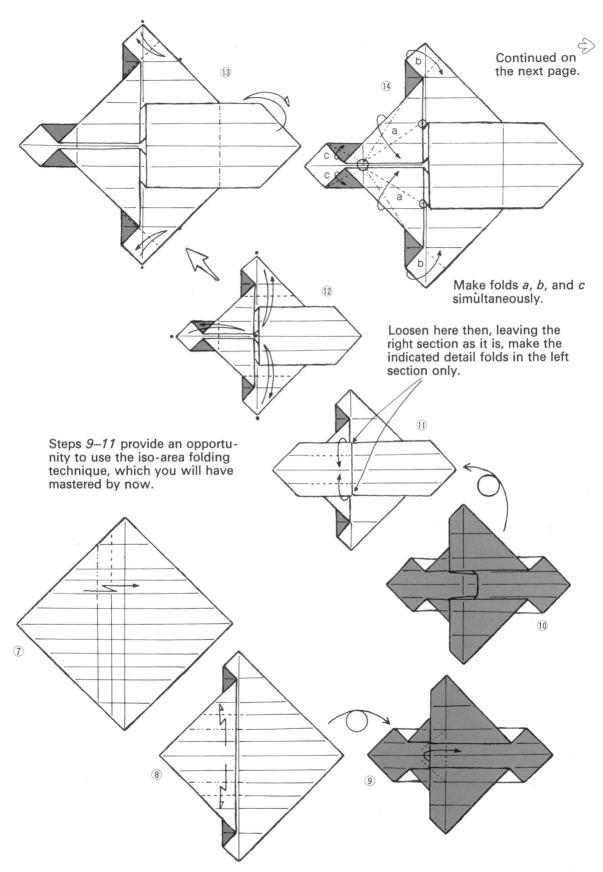

⑬

⑭ b

Continued on
the next page.

a

c c

c c

a

b

Make folds *a*, *b*, and *c*
simùltaneously.

⑫

Loosen here then, leaving the
right section as it is, make the
indicated detail folds in the left
section only.

⑪

Steps *9–11* provide an opportu-
nity to use the iso-area folding
technique, which you will have
mastered by now.

⑩

⑦

⑧

⑨

37

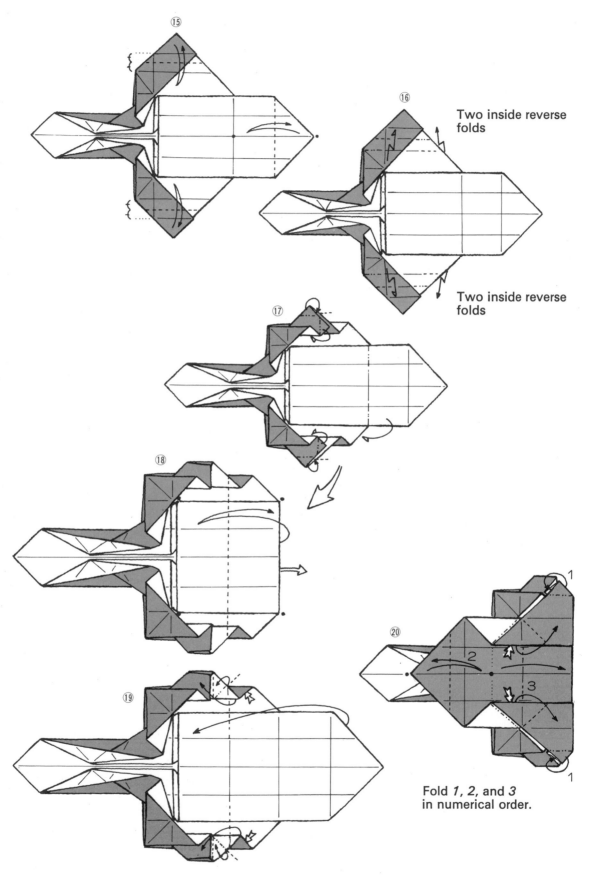

⑮

⑯ Two inside reverse folds

Two inside reverse folds

⑰

⑱

⑲

⑳ Fold *1*, *2*, and *3* in numerical order.

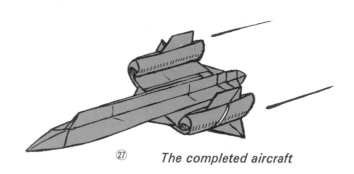

㉗ *The completed aircraft*

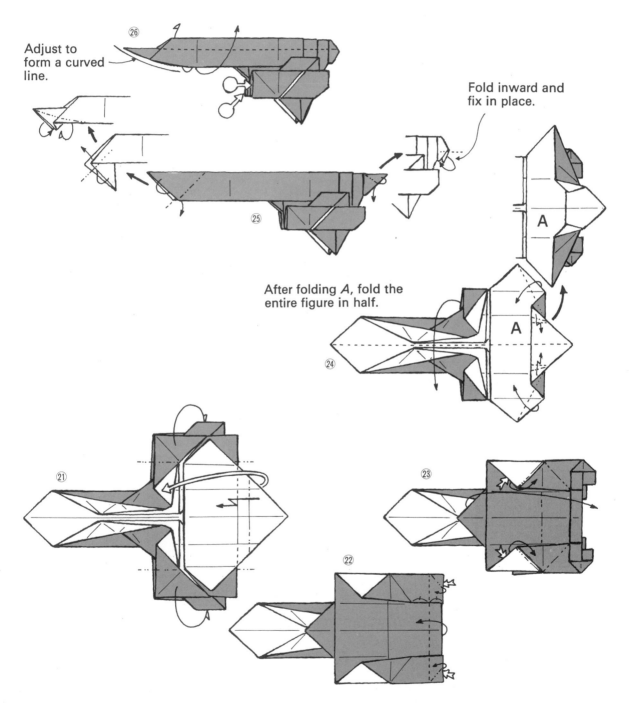

㉖ Adjust to form a curved line.

Fold inward and fix in place.

A

After folding *A*, fold the entire figure in half.

A

㉔

㉕

㉑

㉓

㉒

Space Shuttle

Toshikazu Kawasaki

Another aircraft to follow the SR-71

Using the white side of the paper as the underside is interesting too.

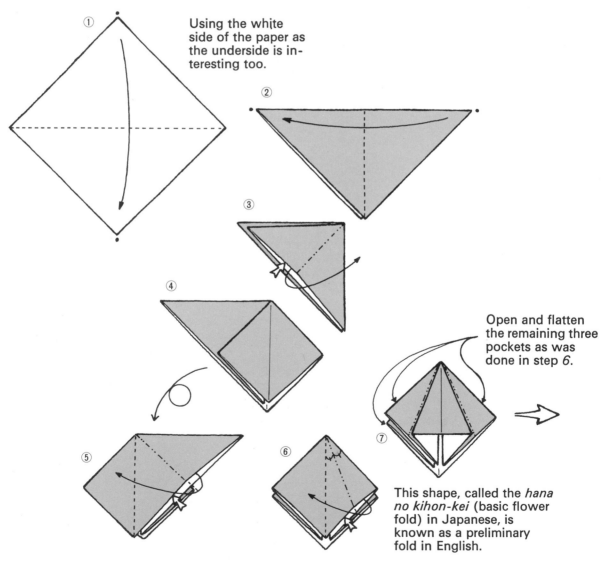

Open and flatten the remaining three pockets as was done in step *6*.

This shape, called the *hana no kihon-kei* (basic flower fold) in Japanese, is known as a preliminary fold in English.

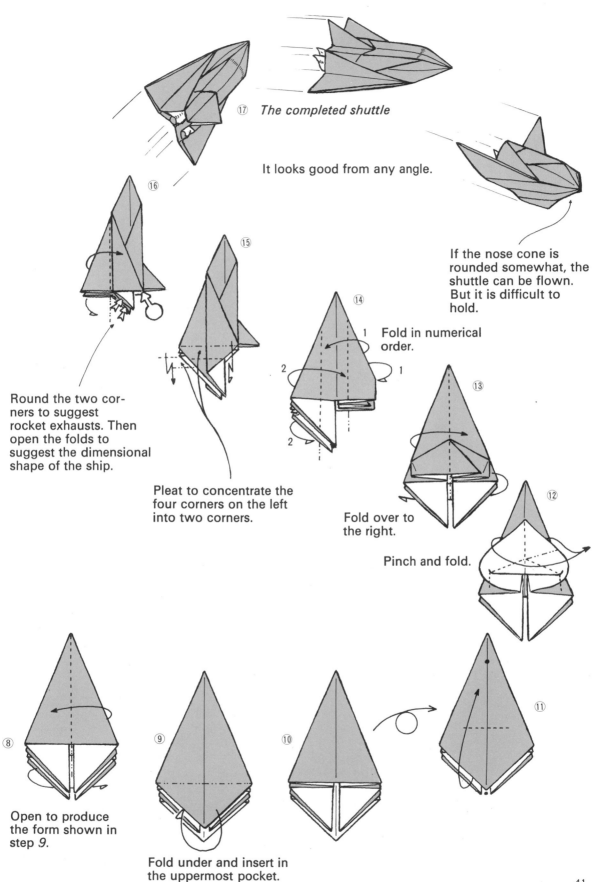

⑰ *The completed shuttle*

It looks good from any angle.

If the nose cone is rounded somewhat, the shuttle can be flown. But it is difficult to hold.

Fold in numerical order.

Round the two corners to suggest rocket exhausts. Then open the folds to suggest the dimensional shape of the ship.

Pleat to concentrate the four corners on the left into two corners.

Fold over to the right.

Pinch and fold.

Open to produce the form shown in step *9*.

Fold under and insert in the uppermost pocket.

Modular Origami

As I said earlier, the ideal of origami is not necessarily folding a form from a single, uncut sheet of paper. Proof of this is to be found in the modular origami works introduced on the following pages. These works begin with a definite form as a goal and invariably involve a number of pieces of paper. Once you have begun making them, you will find them too fascinating to resist.

I begin with the Sonobè Module, which can be called the point of origin of modular origami. Mitsunobu Sonobè, its originator, calls it a *color box;* but I have preferred the conveniently applicable term *Sonobè Module*. The work has already become virtually legendary in popularity.

Little Bird from 38 Units
Kunihiko Kasahara

Sonobè Module

Mitsunobu Sonobè

42

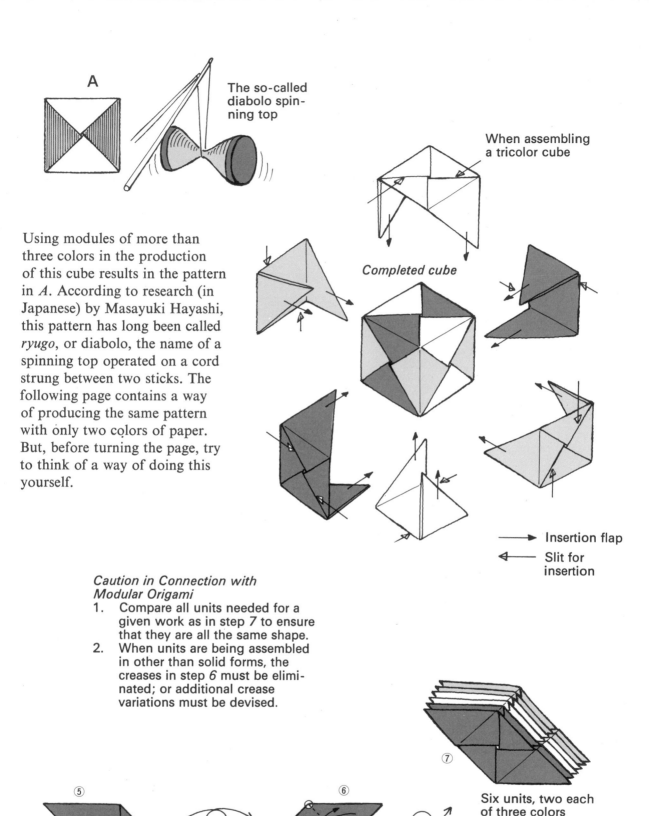

A

The so-called diabolo spinning top

When assembling a tricolor cube

Completed cube

Using modules of more than three colors in the production of this cube results in the pattern in *A*. According to research (in Japanese) by Masayuki Hayashi, this pattern has long been called *ryugo*, or diabolo, the name of a spinning top operated on a cord strung between two sticks. The following page contains a way of producing the same pattern with only two colors of paper. But, before turning the page, try to think of a way of doing this yourself.

→ Insertion flap

⊲— Slit for insertion

Caution in Connection with Modular Origami
1. Compare all units needed for a given work as in step 7 to ensure that they are all the same shape.
2. When units are being assembled in other than solid forms, the creases in step 6 must be eliminated; or additional crease variations must be devised.

⑤

⑥

⑦

Six units, two each of three colors

Simplified Sonobè Module—Bicolor Diabolo Pattern

Kunihiko Kasahara

Of the several possible solutions to the problem, posed on the preceding page, of producing the diabolo pattern with only two colors of paper, the one shown here alters the assembling method and makes use of the different colors of the obverse and reverse sides of the paper.

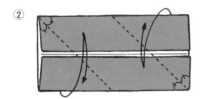

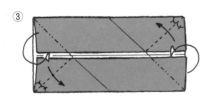

When opened and compared, these two simplified version of the Sonobè Module and the Tomoko Module (p. 68) show that, though the placement of creases in all four is identical, astonishing changes have been produced by varying the use of mountain and valley folds.

Bicolor Diabolo

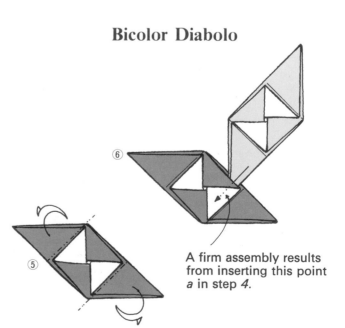

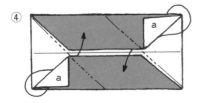

A firm assembly results from inserting this point *a* in step *4*.

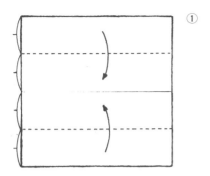

①

②

③

④

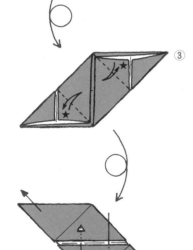

Simple Sonobè System

For an entertaining puzzle, fold the 30-unit multi-modular sphere shown in the photograph above out of three colors of paper and arrange it so that no two adjacent points (pyramids) are of the same color.

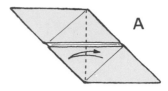

A

In composing a 30-unit modular sphere like the one shown in the photograph below, a fold like the one in *A* is necessary. Further explanations of this topic are forthcoming later.

Multimodular Sphere in 30 Units

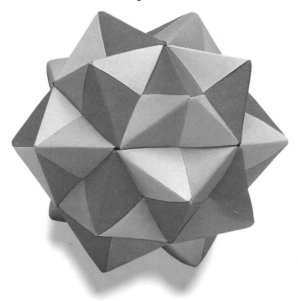

Work on making sure that color duplication does not occur in the pyramidal projections of the 30-unit multimodular sphere shown above. This abbreviated version of the Sonobè module is coarser than the true unit and has several drawbacks. For instance, the corners marked ★ in step *3* tend to get caught and remain outside during the assembly process.

I present it here because it greatly reduces labor for people who are so fascinated by modular origami that they plan works requiring hundreds and even thousands of units (a reduction of 5 processes to 3 constitutes a labor cut of 40 percent). Furthermore, since they are concealed in completed solid forms, the corners that remain sticking out are a problem for only the fastidious.

Exploring the Multimodular Sphere

Although it provided impetus for the spread of modular origami and has by now become so thoroughly established as to be practically a legend, for some reason, no one can recall exactly who first thought up the 30-unit multimodular sphere shown on the preceding page.

First in a trial-and-error manner, our group went on to make 90-unit and 120-unit versions. Then, on the basis of Tokushige Terada's thoughts about the connection between polyhedrons and spheres of this kind, we expanded the upper limit to 300 (at first 270) units, or 10 times the original number.

Reflections on polyhedrons established the need for a secondary unit, the base of which was thought to be limited to a regular hexagon. Further thought about the eighteen polyhedrons shown on page 49, however, showed that regular-octagonal and regular-decagonal bases too were possible.

Relating this idea to the multimodular sphere, with the co-operation of some of his students, Professor Masao Matsuzaki (of the Ikeda Institute of the Osaka University of Education) established tertiary units and increased the possible sphere size to 900 units. A multimodular sphere of that size is shown in the photograph above.

A Primary Module Consisting of 3-*A* Modules

Three Kinds of Secondary Modules Are Conceivable

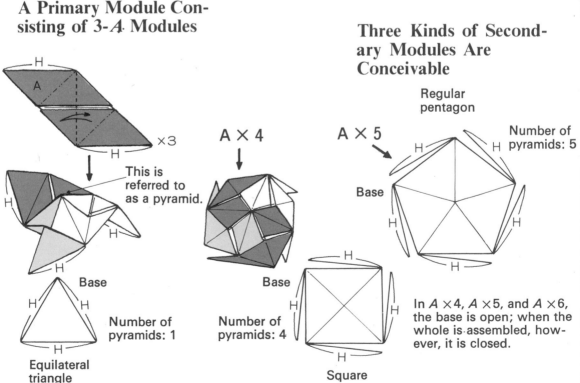

×3

This is referred to as a pyramid.

A × 4

A × 5

Regular pentagon

Number of pyramids: 5

Base

Base

Base

Number of pyramids: 1

Number of pyramids: 4

Equilateral triangle

Square

In *A* ×4, *A* ×5, and *A* ×6, the base is open; when the whole is assembled, however, it is closed.

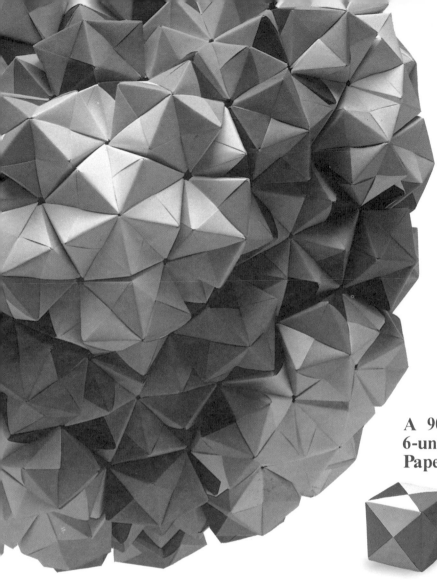

A full week was required to complete the sphere. If this sphere is equated in size with the sun, Jupiter would be about the size of one of the cubes; and Earth would probably be no larger than one of the holes visible on the inside.

A 900-unit Sphere and a 6-unit Cube Made from Paper of the Same Size

Tertiary Unit

Masao Matsuzaki

A group of six $A \times 6$ units (each with six pyramids) is aligned flat on their bases. From this arrangement, other polygonal secondary units (below) were sought. They became the tertiary units.

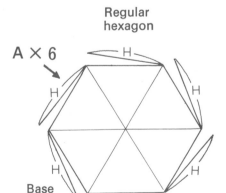

Regular hexagon

$A \times 6$

H H H H H H

Base

Number of pyramids: 6

$A \times 32$

Regular-octagonal base
Number of pyramids: 24

$A \times 40$

Regular-decagonal base
Number of pyramids: 30

47

Polyhedrons and the Multi-modular Sphere

Solid figures, polyhedrons, include the five regular polyhedrons (colored red), in which all faces are the same size and shape, and thirteen semiregular polyhedrons in which the faces differ to an extent. These figures can be realized using the multi-modular system and the secondary and tertiary units introduced on the preceding pages. Try your hand at it.

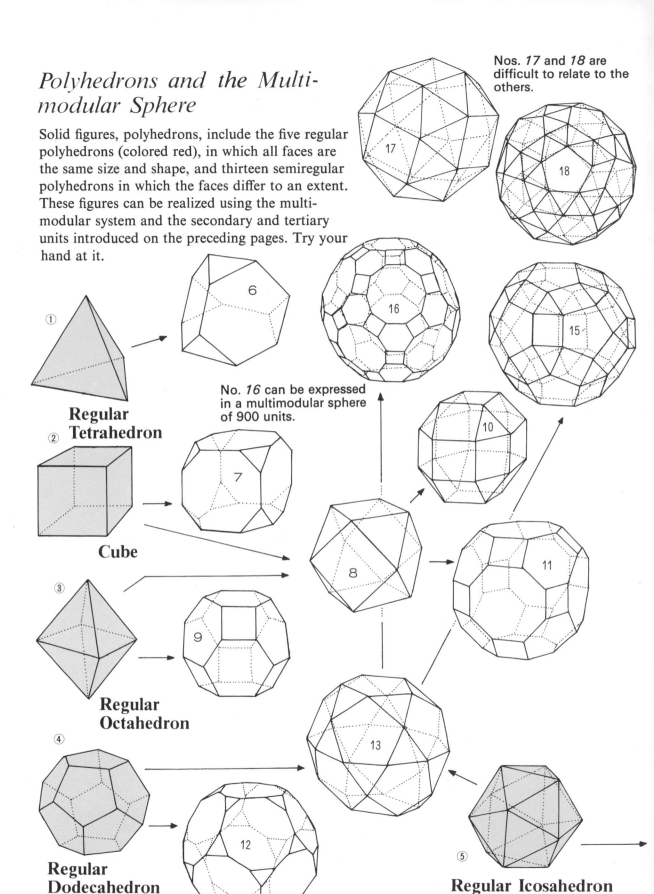

Nos. *17* and *18* are difficult to relate to the others.

No. *16* can be expressed in a multimodular sphere of 900 units.

① **Regular Tetrahedron**

② **Cube**

③ **Regular Octahedron**

④ **Regular Dodecahedron**

⑤ **Regular Icosahedron**

48

No.	Polyhedrons	Forms and Numbers of Forms	Numbers of Units
①	Regular tetrahedron	△ 4	1-a 6 1-b 24
6	Truncated tetrahedron	□ 4 ⬡⟨6⟩ 4	42
②	Hexahedron (cube)	□ 6	36
7	Truncated hexahedron	△ 8 ⬡(8) 6	228
8	Cuboctahedron	△ 8 □ 6	48
③	Octahedron	△ 8	12
9	Truncated octahedron	□ 6 ⟨6⟩ 8	108
10	Rhombicubocta-hedron	△ 8 □ 18	120
11	Rhombitruncated cuboctahedron	□ 12 ⟨6⟩ 8 (8) 6	360
④	Dodecahedron	⬠ 12	90
12	Truncated dodecahedron	△ 20 (10) 12	570
13	Icosidodecahedron	△ 20 ⬠ 12	120
⑤	Icosahedron	△ 20	30
14	Truncated icosahedron	⬠ 12 ⟨6⟩ 20	270
15	Rhombicosidodeca-hedron	△ 20 □ 30 ⬠ 12	300
16	Rhombitruncated icosidodecahedron	□ 30 ⟨6⟩ 20 (10) 12	900
17	Snub cube	△ 32 □ 6	84
18	Snub dodecahedron	△ 80 ⬠ 12	210

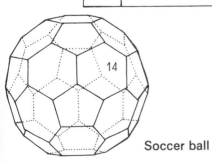

Soccer ball

Since the relation between the 6-unit cube *1-a* and the regular tetrahedron is difficult to understand, I have expanded the one equilateral-triangular face into four pyramids in *1-b*. Both *10* and *13* are composed of 120 units, though their completed forms are different.

Paper Sculpture from Units

How many of the polyhedrons on the preceding page did you succeed in making? Working with geometric forms and units is entertaining because of its variety. Simply altering assembly methods or folds can produce very impressive works. For instance, the multimodular sphere in the photograph above creates a sharp impression because the points are folded with re-entrant angles resulting in tetrahedronal concavities.

Furthermore units can be used in more than geometric forms. For example, their distinctive multidimensional sense produces highly sculpturesque effects in the dog shown below and the horse on the facing page.

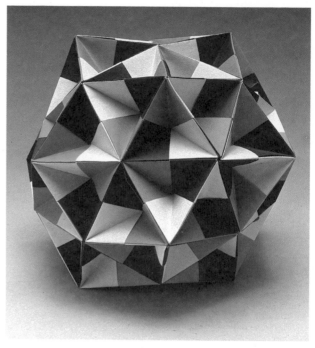

Multimodular Sphere with Re-entrant Angles (90 units of the modified *B* type shown on the facing page)

Dog Made of 84 Units

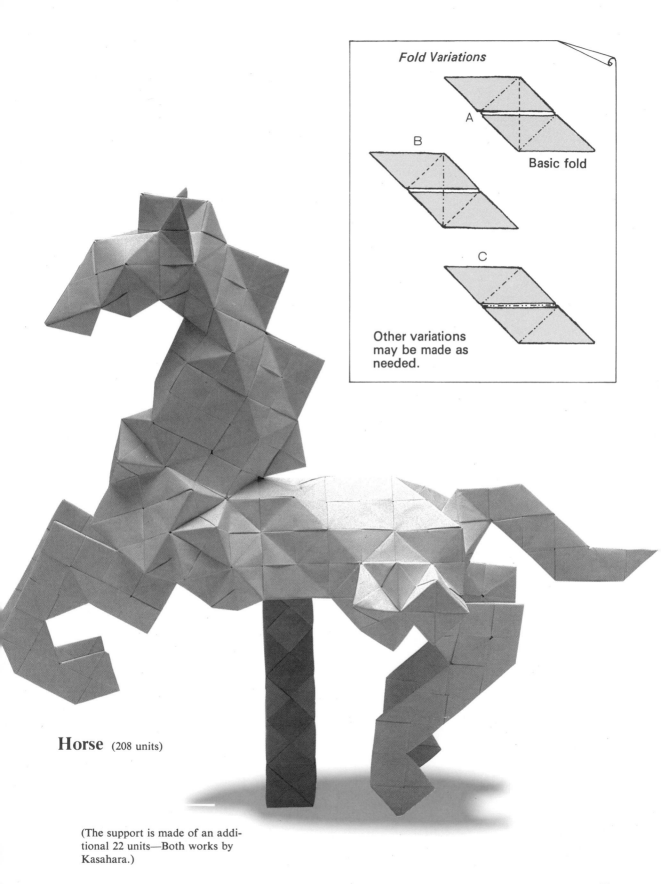

Fold Variations

A

Basic fold

B

C

Other variations
may be made as
needed.

Horse (208 units)

(The support is made of an additional 22 units—Both works by Kasahara.)

Bottle

David Brill

Now, for a change of mood, let us turn
to David Brill for his cellophane bottle,
the appeal of which is greatly enhanced if
something—an origami flower for instance—
is displayed inside. The bottle is made of
one sheet of cellophane; the cap from a
separate piece of paper.

The camellia inside the
bottle too was folded
by David Brill.

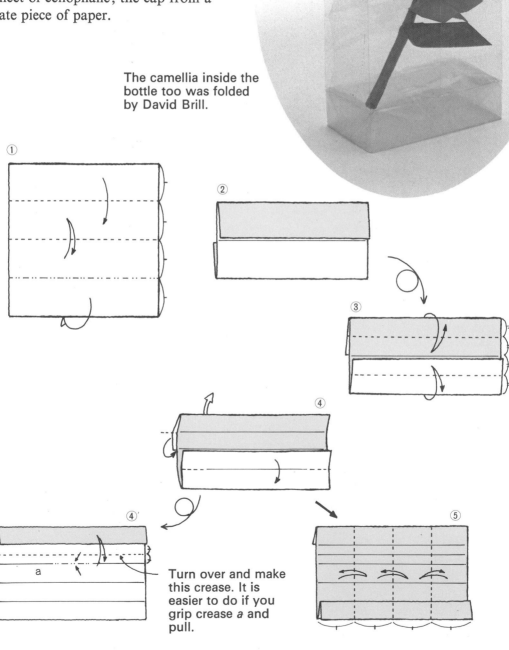

Turn over and make
this crease. It is
easier to do if you
grip crease *a* and
pull.

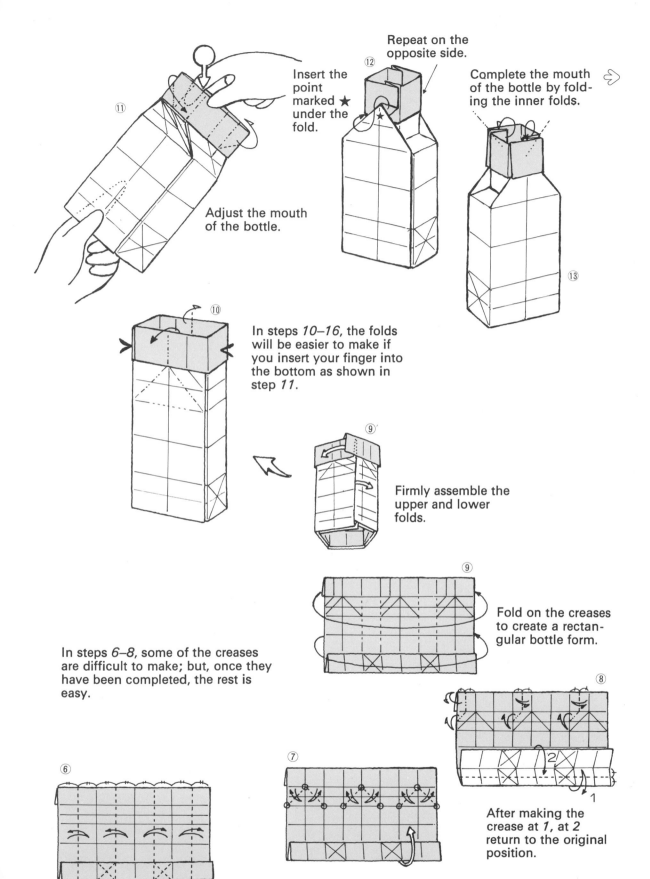

Repeat on the opposite side.

Insert the point marked ★ under the fold.

Complete the mouth of the bottle by folding the inner folds.

Adjust the mouth of the bottle.

In steps *10–16*, the folds will be easier to make if you insert your finger into the bottom as shown in step *11*.

Firmly assemble the upper and lower folds.

Fold on the creases to create a rectangular bottle form.

In steps *6–8*, some of the creases are difficult to make; but, once they have been completed, the rest is easy.

After making the crease at *1*, at *2* return to the original position.

Make two creases at the × marks.

53

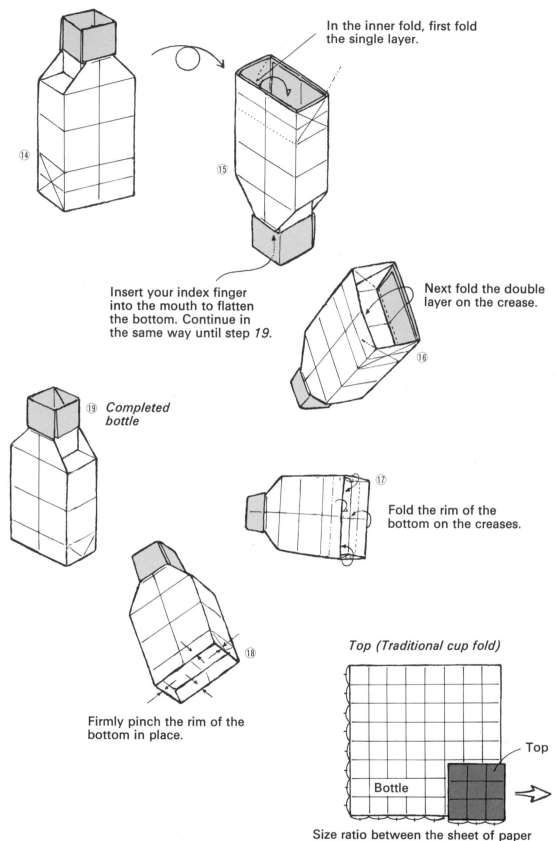

In the inner fold, first fold the single layer.

Insert your index finger into the mouth to flatten the bottom. Continue in the same way until step *19*.

Next fold the double layer on the crease.

⑲ *Completed bottle*

Fold the rim of the bottom on the creases.

Firmly pinch the rim of the bottom in place.

Top (Traditional cup fold)

Top

Bottle

Size ratio between the sheet of paper used for the bottle and the piece (red) used for the top

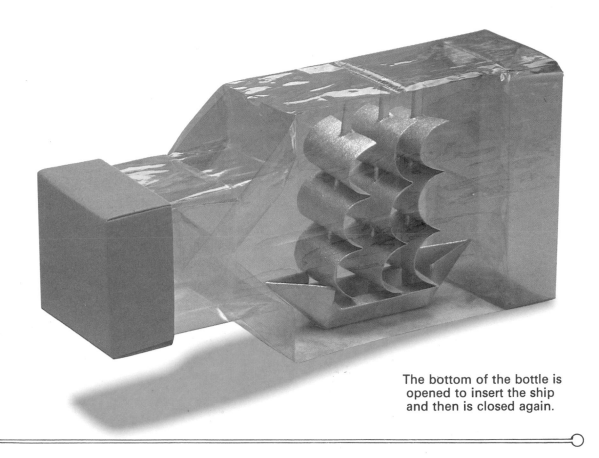

The bottom of the bottle is opened to insert the ship and then is closed again.

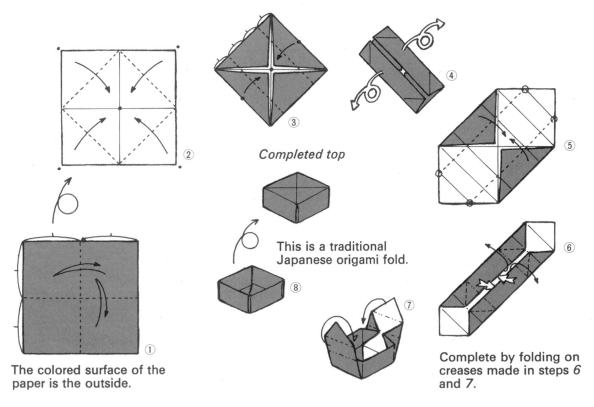

② ③

Completed top

This is a traditional Japanese origami fold.

④ ⑤ ⑥ ⑦ ⑧

① The colored surface of the paper is the outside.

Complete by folding on creases made in steps *6* and *7*.

Regular Polyhedrons from Single Sheets of Square Paper

Kazuo Haga

The five regular polyhedrons, all of whose faces are of the same shape and size, might appear to be simple but are actually extremely difficult to fold, especially from single sheets of square paper. Among them, the regular dodecahedron, which is based on the regular pentagon, is extremely demanding. Kazuo Haga, a professor of biology at Tsukuba University, addressed himself to this problem for his own amusement and did an excellent job of overcoming its difficulties.

As has already been seen from various actual applications of them, the regular tetrahedron, hexahedron, and octahedron are relatively simple. Professor Haga's system is the only one developed so far, however, for folding the more difficult icosahedron and dodecahedron from single square sheets of paper. Before turning to the explanatory drawings, examine the photographs of these two figures, on the right, and give some thought to the relation between them and the square.

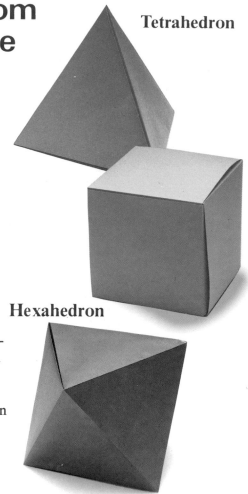

Tetrahedron

Hexahedron

Octahedron

Tetrahedron

Independently invented by Haga, Kasahara, and Maekawa

① Do no more than make crease marks.

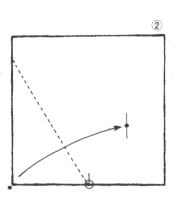

②

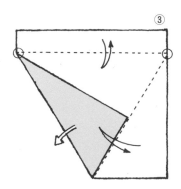

③

Dodecahedron

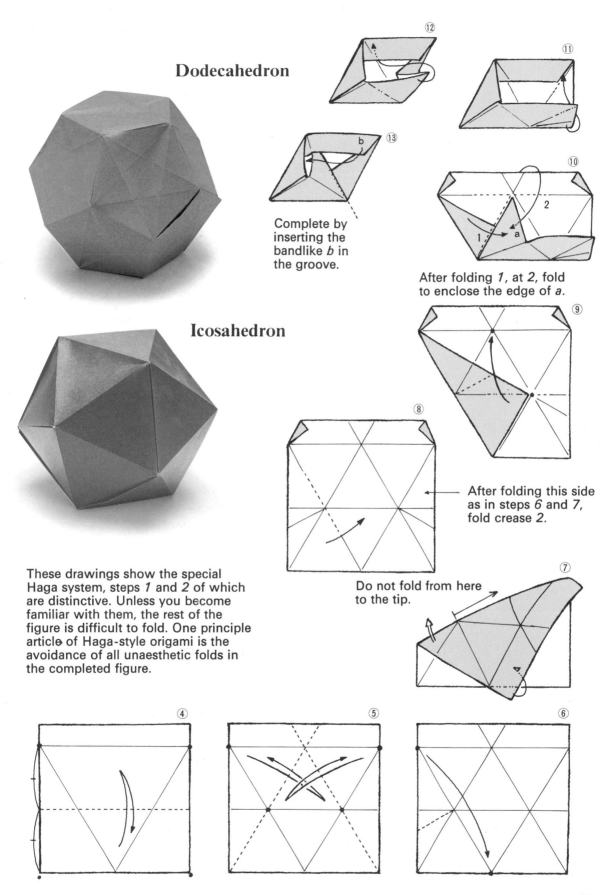

⑫

⑪

⑬

Complete by
inserting the
bandlike *b* in
the groove.

⑩

After folding *1*, at *2*, fold
to enclose the edge of *a*.

Icosahedron

⑨

⑧

After folding this side
as in steps *6* and *7*,
fold crease *2*.

These drawings show the special
Haga system, steps *1* and *2* of which
are distinctive. Unless you become
familiar with them, the rest of the
figure is difficult to fold. One principle
article of Haga-style origami is the
avoidance of all unaesthetic folds in
the completed figure.

⑦

Do not fold from here
to the tip.

④ ⑤ ⑥

The HK Cube, or Trick Dice

Independently invented by Haga and Kasahara

On the preceding page, I mentioned one of the basic articles on which the origami of Kazuo Haga is founded. Though I do not advocate that everyone abide by them, I will introduce all five articles of his credo because they interestingly reveal much about his personality.

1. The production of geometrical figures with single sheets of unadorned origami paper.
2. Use only the hands; no tools of any kind are permitted.
3. No cutting or tearing is permitted; it must be possible to unfold the paper to its original form.
4. The figures produced must be sturdy and stable.
5. The completed figure must be well-finished and elegant.

The insistence on unadorned paper suggests the shyness a college teacher feels about playing with the kind of colored sheets children use. It is scholarly of Haga to restrict himself to geometric forms.

Perhaps at a glance these restrictions seem severe, but I sense a humorous note in them. Making the cube into a trick die was a Kasahara idea.

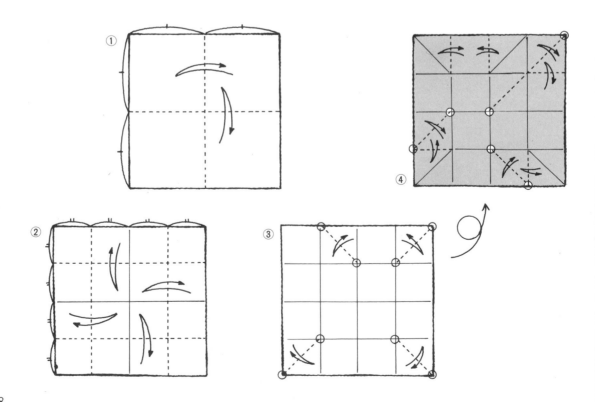

58

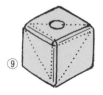

Putting dots on the paper as shown below at step *4*, before the solid is assembled, produces a trick die. Because of the added weight resulting from numerous folds of paper at the face marked with one dot, the face with six dots is likely to come up on top when the die is thrown.

Because I am unable to present a set of drawings accurately representing the Haga cube, I introduce the Kasahara version. Though it may differ slightly from the Haga one, it conforms to his five rules. In other words, the two of us have arrived at our own solutions to the same problem.

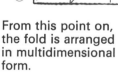

⑤

From this point on, the fold is arranged in multidimensional form.

Completed cube

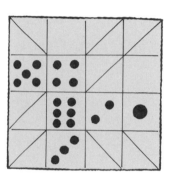

⑨

Insert the three corners into the facing pockets.

⑧

Arrange on the basis of the creases.

The corner marked ★ must be bent around beneath *a*.

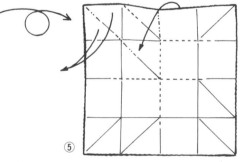

⑥

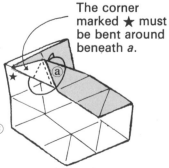

⑦

Octahedron

Kazuo Haga

As is true in the cases of the regular tetrahedron and the cube as well, a number of versions have been developed for folding the regular octahedron. But Haga's is the most perfect. There are no unwanted creases in the finished form, and the folding method after step *8* is pleasingly rhythmical. Folded perfectly flat until just before completion, the figure is suddenly and amusingly given multidimensional form. After you have learned how, you will probably want to make a number of these octahedrons, which can be suspended on threads as elegant mobiles.

The folding begins as for the regular tetrahedron shown on page 56.

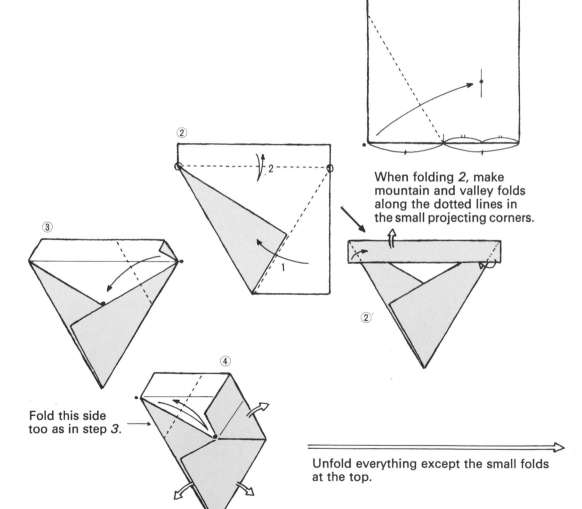

When folding *2*, make mountain and valley folds along the dotted lines in the small projecting corners.

Fold this side too as in step *3*.

Unfold everything except the small folds at the top.

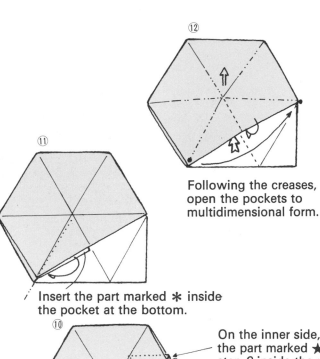

Following the creases, open the pockets to multidimensional form.

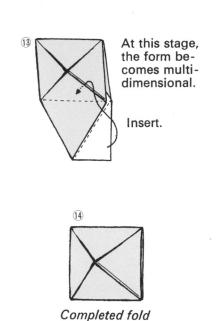

At this stage, the form becomes multi-dimensional.

Insert.

⑭

Completed fold

⑪

Insert the part marked ✳ inside the pocket at the bottom.

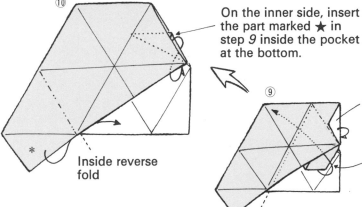

On the inner side, insert the part marked ★ in step *9* inside the pocket at the bottom.

Inside reverse fold

Following the creases, fold this inner part completely inward.

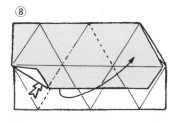

No new creases are made after step 7.

In steps *5* and *6*, make new creases that are extensions or are based on the creases made up to step *4*.

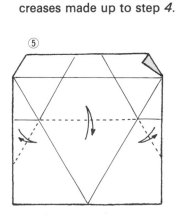

⑥

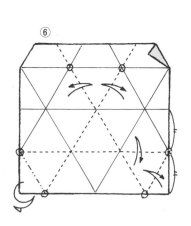

⑦

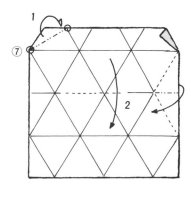

61

Icosahedron

Kazuo Haga

Though they all look the same in the photograph, each of the three icosahedrons is folded in a different way.

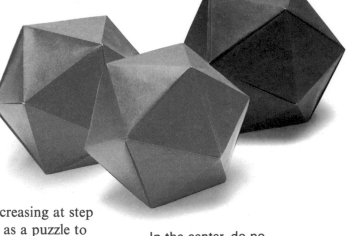

You have probably easily mastered the three preceding solid figures. The icosahedron is much more difficult. Furthermore, it is hard to explain with drawings. All steps up to the creasing at step *8* are very clear. Regard the final assembly as a puzzle to be worked out on your own.

The version I present is slightly different after step *9* from Haga's icosahedron. Not intended as improvements, the changes have been adopted to make the figure somewhat easier to demonstrate in drawings.

In the center, do no more than make a crease mark.

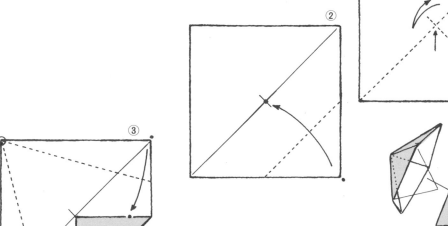

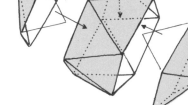

A

The creases form a regular hexagon within the square of the sheet of paper.

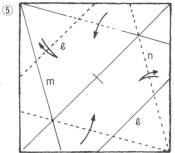

Unfold and repeat the folds in steps *2* and *3* from the opposite side.

In the Haga assembly method (shown on the far right), *A* and *A'* are aligned to form a pocket, into which *A''* is inserted. Similarly *B* and *B'* are aligned to form a pocket, into which *B''* is inserted. The arrangement is essentially tripartite.

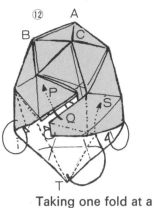

⑫

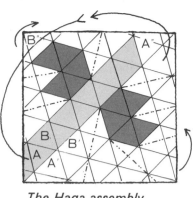

The Haga assembly

Taking one fold at a time, insert *T* into *S* and *Q* into *P*.

Assembly at this stage

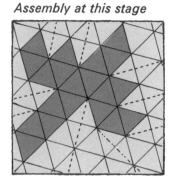

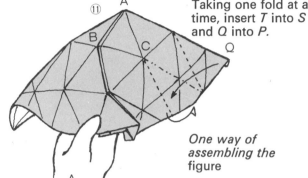

⑪

One way of assembling the figure

The four intersections marked ○ are not aligned with the edges.

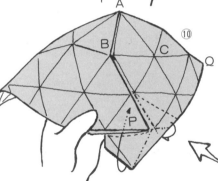

⑩

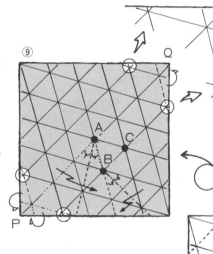

⑨

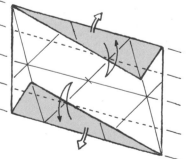

⑧

Intermediate steps not shown.

Next fold *m* and *n* in step *5*. Then fold as in steps *6* and *7*. Then, using *l* as a guide, fold to divide the whole sheet into eight equal parts.

Fold so as to align the two edges.

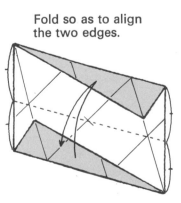

Fold so as to align the edges with the creases.

⑦

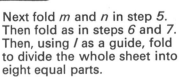

Dodecahedron

Kazuo Haga

The dodecahedron is even more difficult than the admittedly hard icosahedron. Making a stable icosahedron without glue and with no more than a single sheet of paper is possible but extremely demanding. Consequently, here I have limited the presentation to the very simple, regular pentagon, which makes use of the Haga Theorem (p. 18) and a plan drawing of the dodecahedron. But the plan is a very clear indication of the way to produce this highly sophisticated figure.

When using paper 6 in (15 cm) to a side, allow point *P* to project 1/16–1/8 in (2–3 mm) above the edge to the left of midpoint. Using the edge of the paper as a guide, fold *a*.

Midpoint

① P

a

Hold the paper in place by pressing a finger on the spot marked ○ as you fold *a*.

Do not crease here.

These two edges should be perfectly aligned.

②

③′

③

I have selected the most convenient of the various different methods for accurately (theoretically, zero error) folding a regular pentagon.

⑥

④

⑤

Plan Drawing for a Dodecahedron

Original drawing by Kazuo Haga

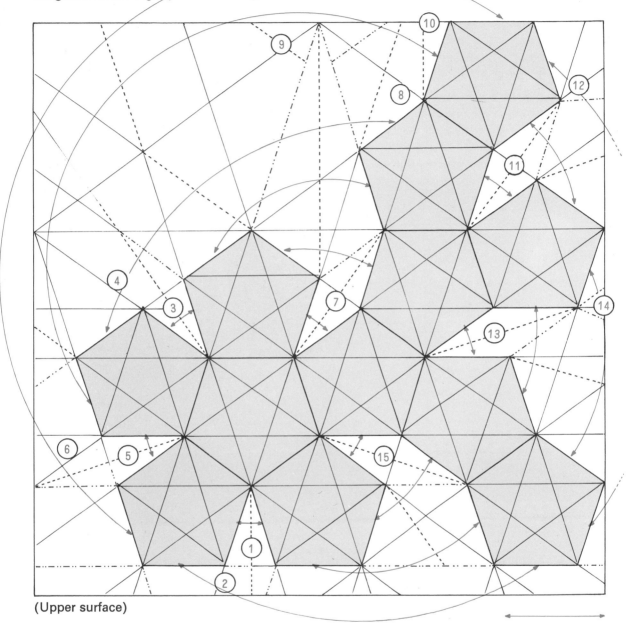

(Upper surface)

Outlines that come into mutual contact

Additional lines

- People who want to do everything in a hurry can have a copy made of this drawing and fold from the copy.
- Numbers in circles indicate folding order. The twelve red pentagons will be the faces of the dodecahedron. All of their perimeters are mountain folds.
- Lines connecting the points of the regular pentagon in step *6* on the facing page inscribe a small pentagon within the larger one. Extending the diagonal lines of the small pentagon generates other small pentagons that result in the figure shown above.
- Once the requisite twelve pentagons have been formed, additional, nonstructural lines may be added to produce a star pattern in each face.

65

The Limitless Appeal of the Cube

As I said at the outset, geometric forms tend to arouse little interest; and perhaps the most apparently plebeian and least appealing is the cube. But reexamination after experience with many other solid forms reveals the cube to possess limitless appeal and unexpected aspects. Large showy blossoms are beautiful, but the perceptive eye can be smitten with the beauty of the small, modest, pathside flower too. At this point, I should like to present still more examples of the cube in interesting variations.

The Fujimoto Cube

Shuzo Fujimoto

Shuzo Fujimoto is both a pioneer in the practical introduction of geometric forms to the world of origami and in their use as teaching material in explaining molecular structure to high-school science classes. Both his books and several of his origami works are widely known and enjoyed among researchers. Since this famous cube, which an English research worker has described as a poem, is indispensable to any discussion of the charm of origami, I have included it here. It will enable you to savor the pleasure and wonder of origami to the full.

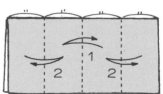

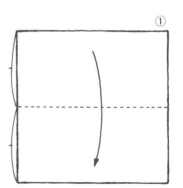

Fold in numerical order.

66

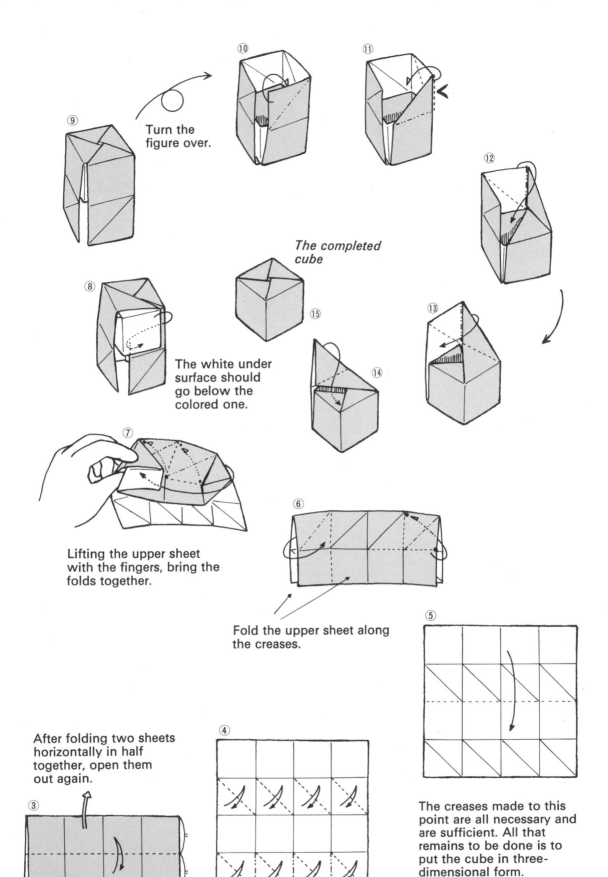

Turn the figure over.

The completed cube

The white under surface should go below the colored one.

Lifting the upper sheet with the fingers, bring the folds together.

Fold the upper sheet along the creases.

After folding two sheets horizontally in half together, open them out again.

The creases made to this point are all necessary and are sufficient. All that remains to be done is to put the cube in three-dimensional form.

The Hosoya Cube—Folding Two Components and Then Assembling Them to Make a Cube

Haruo Hosoya

Please do not consider it a technological regression to use two sheets of paper to form a cube after having learned how to fold a splendid one from a single sheet.

The paper is divided into three equal parts as shown on page 26.

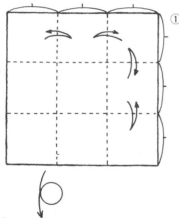

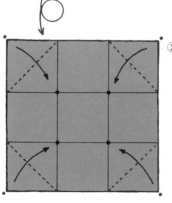

Whereas the Fujimoto cube represents a superb folding order, the Hosoya cube is a superlative idea. Both Haruo Hosoya, who teaches at the Ochanomizu Women's College, and Shuzo Fujimoto employ origami in the classroom to explain molecular and crystal structures.

The great charm of origami made from two sheets of paper is the possibility of color combinations. Although it is possible to make bicolor origami like the Kawasaki cube (pp. 30–35) by employing the obverse and reverse sides of a single sheet of paper, the process is complicated. The topic is not dealt with in this book, but I think you would derive considerable pleasure from thinking about origami made with three sheets of paper.

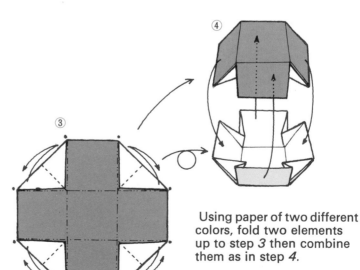

Using paper of two different colors, fold two elements up to step *3* then combine them as in step *4*.

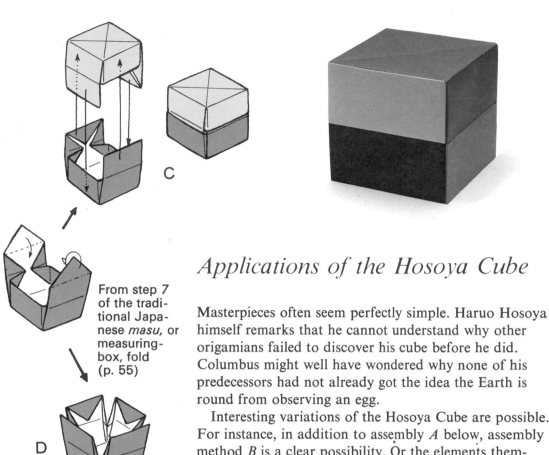

C

From step 7 of the traditional Japanese *masu*, or measuring-box, fold (p. 55)

D

Applications of the Hosoya Cube

Masterpieces often seem perfectly simple. Haruo Hosoya himself remarks that he cannot understand why other origamians failed to discover his cube before he did. Columbus might well have wondered why none of his predecessors had not already got the idea the Earth is round from observing an egg.

Interesting variations of the Hosoya Cube are possible. For instance, in addition to assembly *A* below, assembly method *B* is a clear possibility. Or the elements themselves may be varied, as is shown on the left, into the traditional Japanese *masu* or measuring-box form, which may be easily combined as in *C*, which produces a slightly larger cube that is conveniently the same size as the 6-unit cube (pp. 42–44).

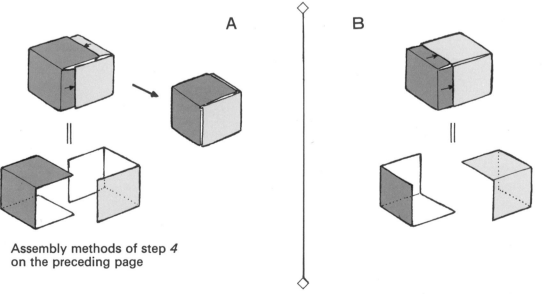

A

B

Assembly methods of step *4* on the preceding page

The Tomoko Unit

Tomoko Fusè

Now let us reexamine the 6-unit cube. In connection with the work on the facing page, I suggest that you use six sheets of paper of different colors.

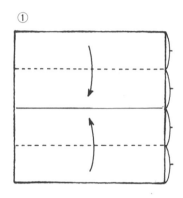

As can be seen in *A* below, not one, but two slits may may be used for connections in this version. Consequently, if the upper layer in step *6* is folded inward, assembly at two points is possible. The cube shown above was made in this way. For other assembly variations see page 25.

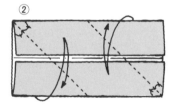

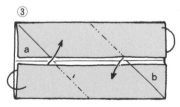

Pull out corners *a* and *b*, visible in step *3*, and make outside reverse folds.

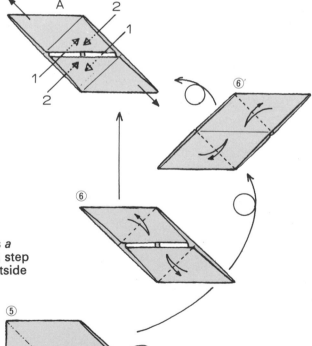

Rotating Ring of Cubes

Hisashi Matsumoto

Not an origami work, this rotating ring of cubes is an appealing patented idea, one of several similar ones that Professor Hisashi Matsumoto (Yokohama National University) has developed for use in teaching cube-related forms to primary- and middle-school pupils. It makes good use of the Tomoko unit.

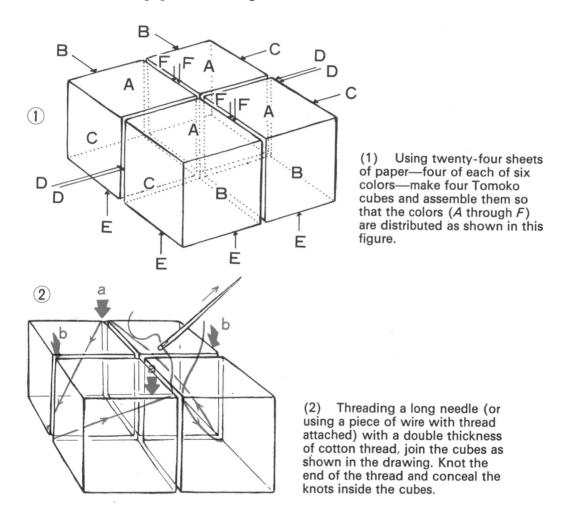

(1)   Using twenty-four sheets of paper—four of each of six colors—make four Tomoko cubes and assemble them so that the colors (*A* through *F*) are distributed as shown in this figure.

(2)   Threading a long needle (or using a piece of wire with thread attached) with a double thickness of cotton thread, join the cubes as shown in the drawing. Knot the end of the thread and conceal the knots inside the cubes.

The cubes may be rotated, revealing different-colored faces, by tapping them lightly with finger on points *a* or *b*. Still greater pleasure and color variation results from replacing these cubes with patterned Rotating Tetrahedrons (p. 16).

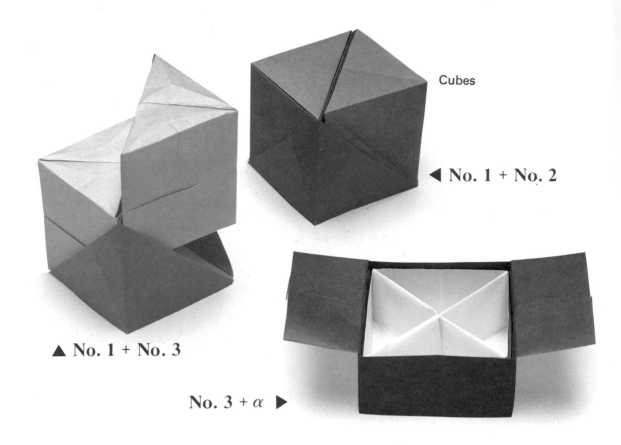

Cubes

◀ **No. 1 + No. 2**

▲ **No. 1 + No. 3**

No. 3 + α ▶

Seven Geometric Forms

Jun Maekawa

You will appreciate the uniqueness of their folding methods as you actually produce the seven new geometric forms by Jun Maekawa presented here.

Model No. 1 (Cubic carrying box of a traditional kind called *okamochi*

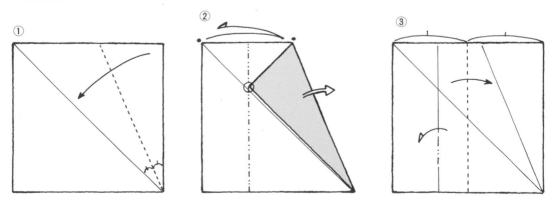

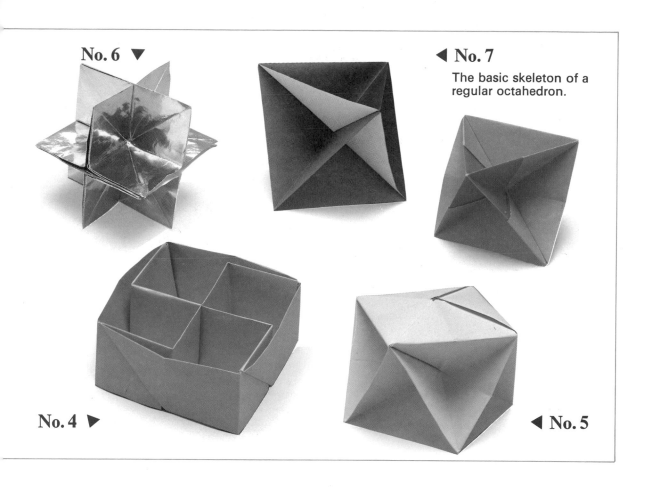

No. 6 ▼

◄ No. 7

The basic skeleton of a
regular octahedron.

No. 4 ▶

◄ No. 5

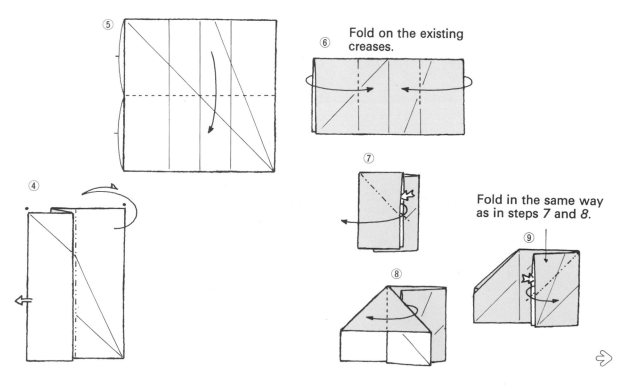

⑤

⑥ Fold on the existing
creases.

④

⑦

Fold in the same way
as in steps *7* and *8*.

⑧

⑨

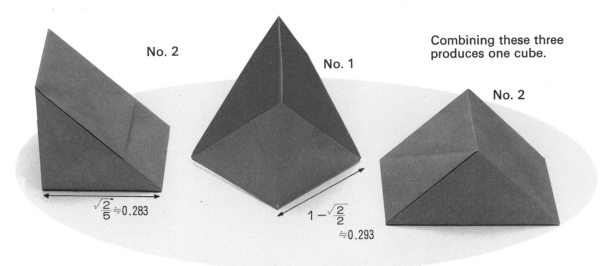

No. 2

No. 1

No. 2

Combining these three produces one cube.

$$\frac{\sqrt{2}}{5} \doteq 0.283$$

$$1 - \frac{\sqrt{2}}{2} \doteq 0.293$$

Model No. 2 (Half a cube)

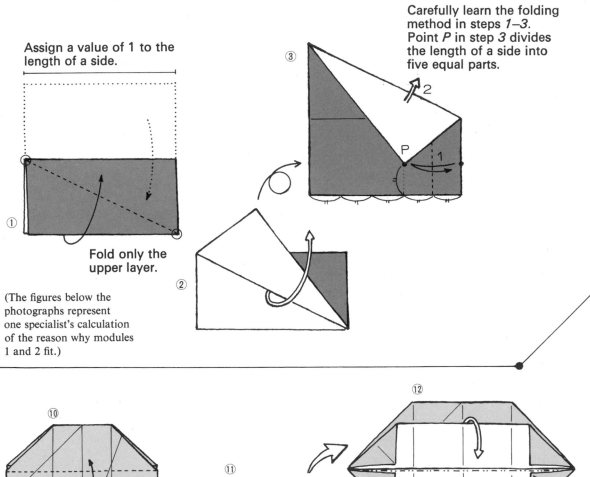

Assign a value of 1 to the length of a side.

①

Fold only the upper layer.

②

(The figures below the photographs represent one specialist's calculation of the reason why modules 1 and 2 fit.)

③

Carefully learn the folding method in steps *1–3*. Point *P* in step *3* divides the length of a side into five equal parts.

P

2

1

⑩

⑪

⑫

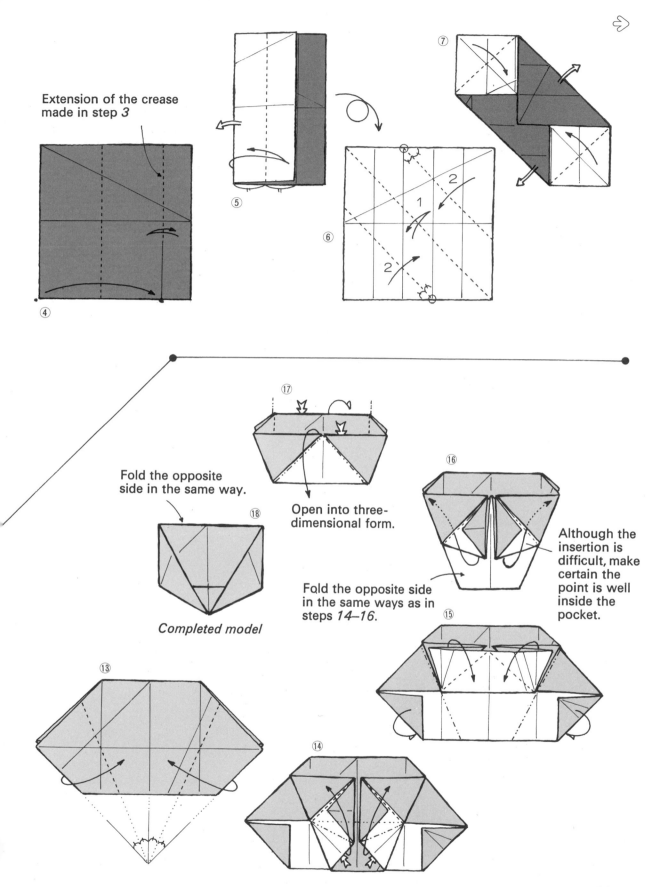

Extension of the crease
made in step *3*

Fold the opposite
side in the same way.

Open into three-
dimensional form.

Fold the opposite side
in the same ways as in
steps *14–16*.

Although the
insertion is
difficult, make
certain the
point is well
inside the
pocket.

Completed model

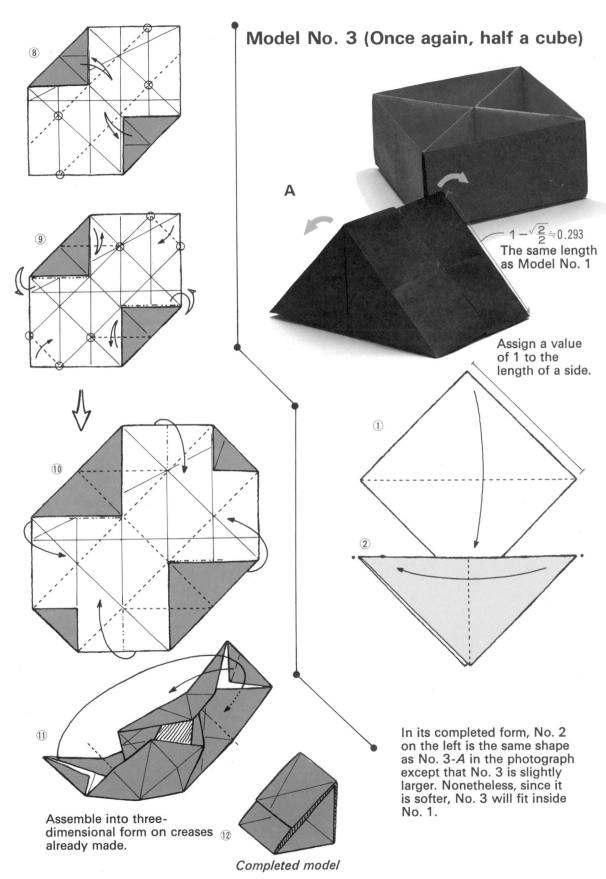

Model No. 3 (Once again, half a cube)

A

$1 - \dfrac{\sqrt{2}}{2} \fallingdotseq 0.293$

The same length as Model No. 1

Assign a value of 1 to the length of a side.

⑧

⑨

⑩

⑪ Assemble into three-dimensional form on creases already made.

⑫ *Completed model*

①

②

In its completed form, No. 2 on the left is the same shape as No. 3-*A* in the photograph except that No. 3 is slightly larger. Nonetheless, since it is softer, No. 3 will fit inside No. 1.

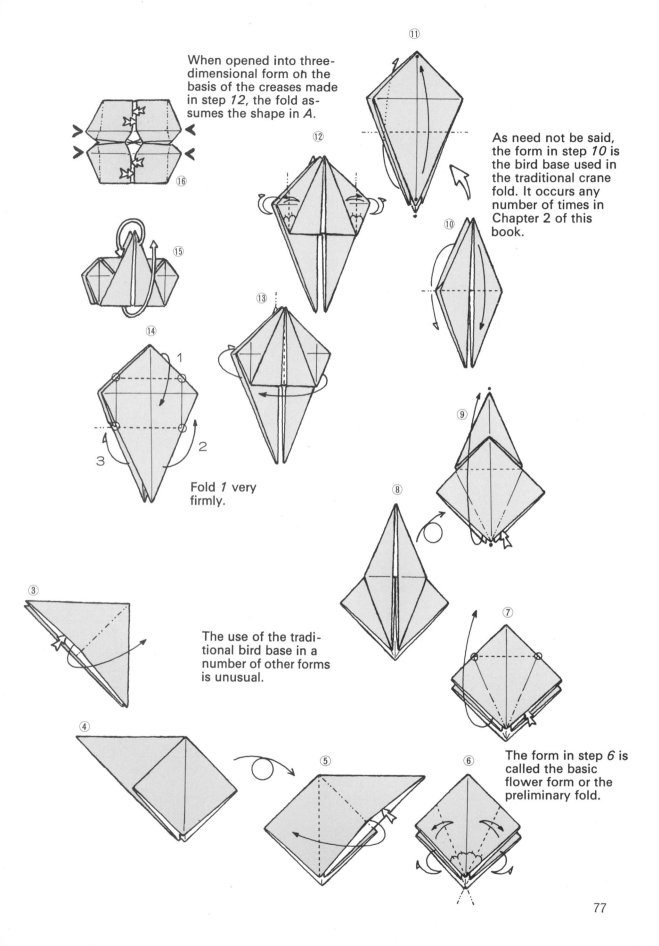

When opened into three-dimensional form on the basis of the creases made in step *12*, the fold assumes the shape in *A*.

⑯

⑪

As need not be said, the form in step *10* is the bird base used in the traditional crane fold. It occurs any number of times in Chapter 2 of this book.

⑫

⑮

⑩

⑬

⑭

Fold *1* very firmly.

1

2

3

⑨

⑧

The use of the traditional bird base in a number of other forms is unusual.

⑦

③

④

⑤

⑥

The form in step *6* is called the basic flower form or the preliminary fold.

Model No. 4 (Divided *masu* measuring box)

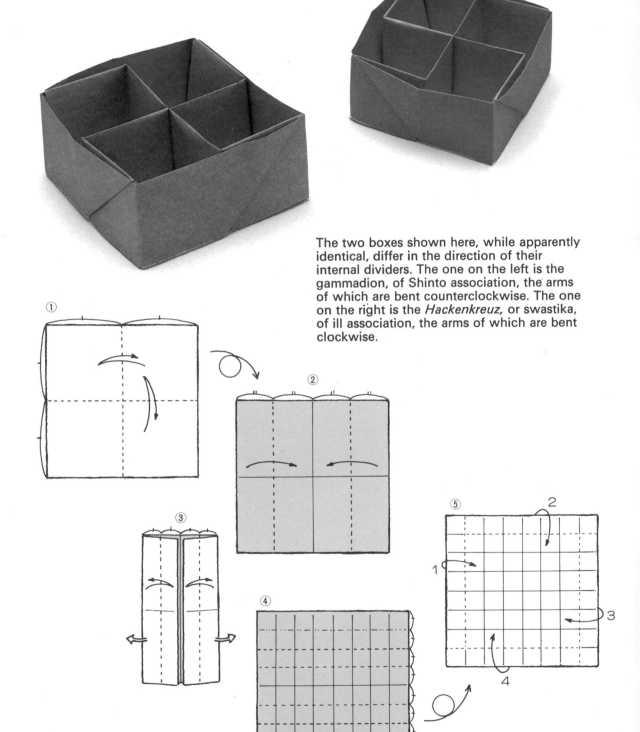

The two boxes shown here, while apparently identical, differ in the direction of their internal dividers. The one on the left is the gammadion, of Shinto association, the arms of which are bent counterclockwise. The one on the right is the *Hackenkreuz,* or swastika, of ill association, the arms of which are bent clockwise.

Steps *2* and *3* divided the sheet vertically into eighths. Now fold so as to divide it horizontally into eighths.

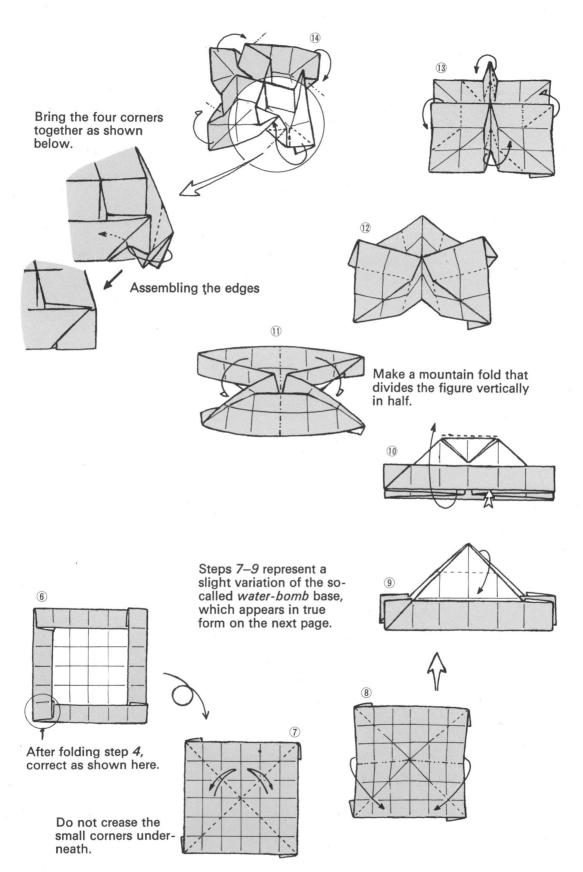

Bring the four corners together as shown below.

Assembling the edges

Make a mountain fold that divides the figure vertically in half.

Steps *7–9* represent a slight variation of the so-called *water-bomb* base, which appears in true form on the next page.

After folding step *4*, correct as shown here.

Do not crease the small corners underneath.

⑥ ⑦ ⑧ ⑨ ⑩ ⑪ ⑫ ⑬ ⑭

Model No. 5 (Semiregular decahedron with some reentrant corners)

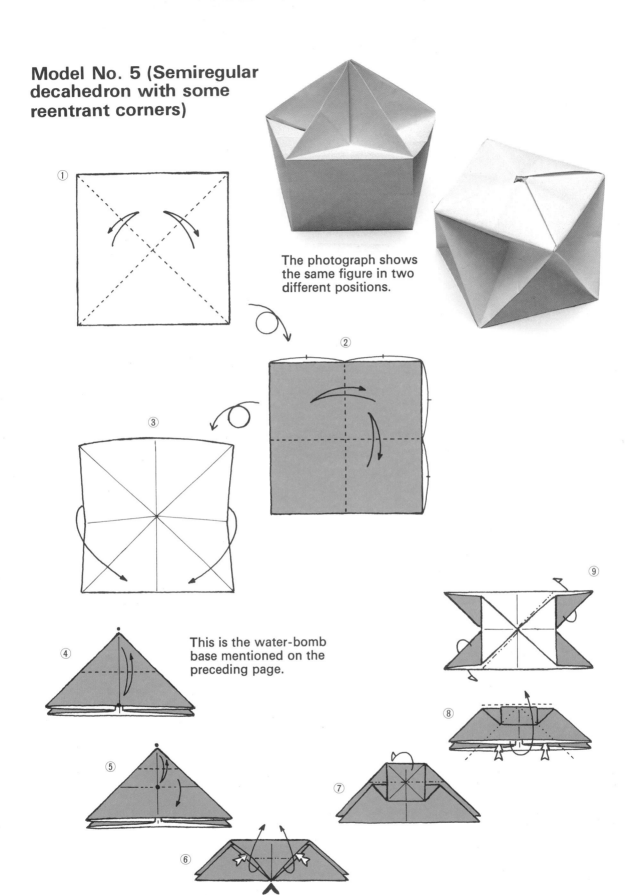

The photograph shows the same figure in two different positions.

This is the water-bomb base mentioned on the preceding page.

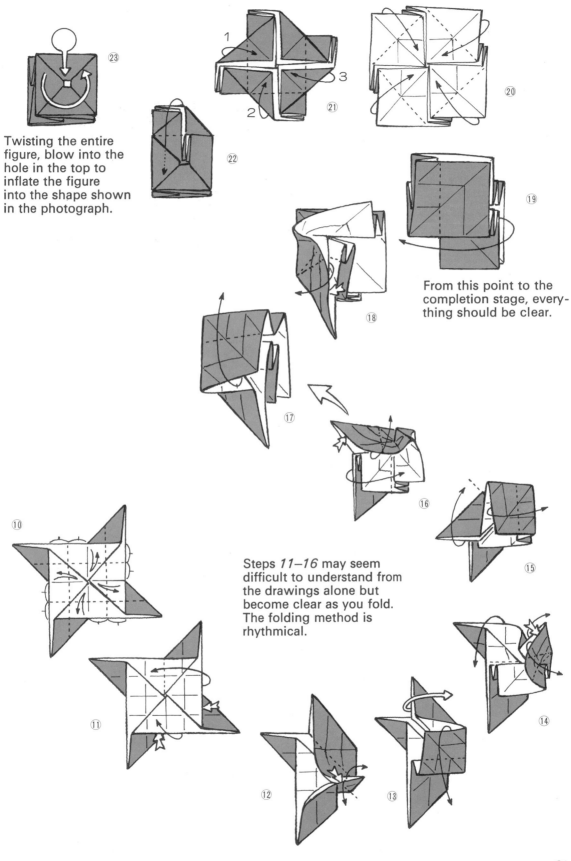

㉓

Twisting the entire
figure, blow into the
hole in the top to
inflate the figure
into the shape shown
in the photograph.

㉒

1
2
3
㉑

㉕

㉑

㉓

㉙ From this point to the
completion stage, every-
thing should be clear.

㉘

㉗

㉖

㉕

Steps 11–16 may seem
difficult to understand from
the drawings alone but
become clear as you fold.
The folding method is
rhythmical.

⑩

⑪

⑫

⑬

⑭

81

Model No. 6

Four interpenetrating square sheets.
Compare this with the skeleton of
the regular octahedron (p. 33).
This model is clean and sharp when
folded with large sheets of thin paper.

①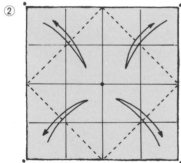

This figure is used in explaining the
Cartesian coordinates of planes intersecting each other at right angles. Seen from
another vantage point, it suggests the cube
skeleton structure. The photograph on the
right is of a Model No. 6 fitted inside a
Fujimoto Cube (p. 66) made of cellophane.

At step *5*, crease
only the upper layer
without making folds
in the small square
underneath.

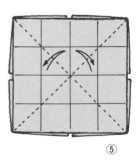

⑤

②

③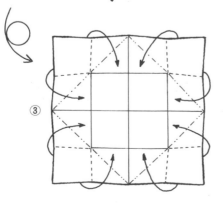

④

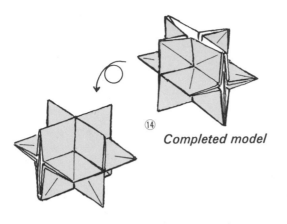

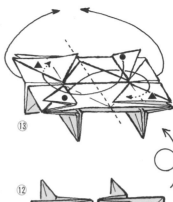

Fold vertically in half. Insert the corner marked ● beneath the corner marked ▲.

⑬

⑭ *Completed model*

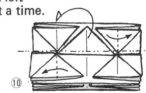

⑫

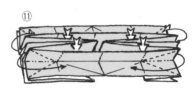

Raise the central part to produce the figure seen in step *12*.

⑥

Make inside reverse folds at the inner folds.

⑦

Fold right and left corners one at a time.

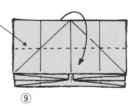

⑩

Fold half only down.

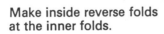

⑧

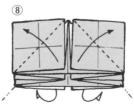

⑨

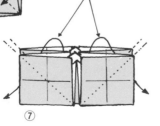

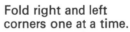

83

Model No. 7 (Iso-area folding)

Many people have worked variations on this skeleton of the regular octahedron. Four variations by Jun Maekawa are shown in the photograph at the bottom of the facing page. The one shown here employs the iso-area folding method that came into being after the initial encounter between Kawasaki and Maekawa.

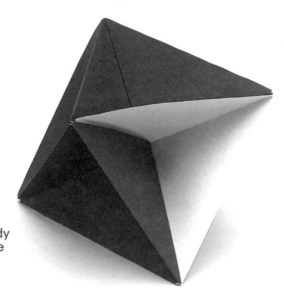

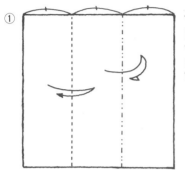

You should already have mastered the way of folding paper into equal thirds.

Although it is not apparent in the photograph, the completely equal amount of revealed upper and under surface produces a startling impression.

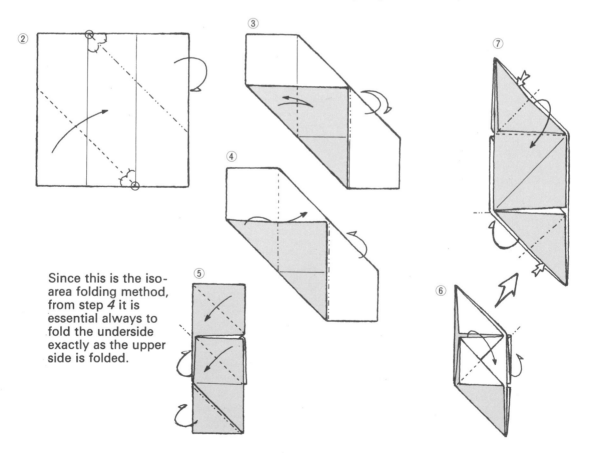

Since this is the iso-area folding method, from step 4 it is essential always to fold the underside exactly as the upper side is folded.

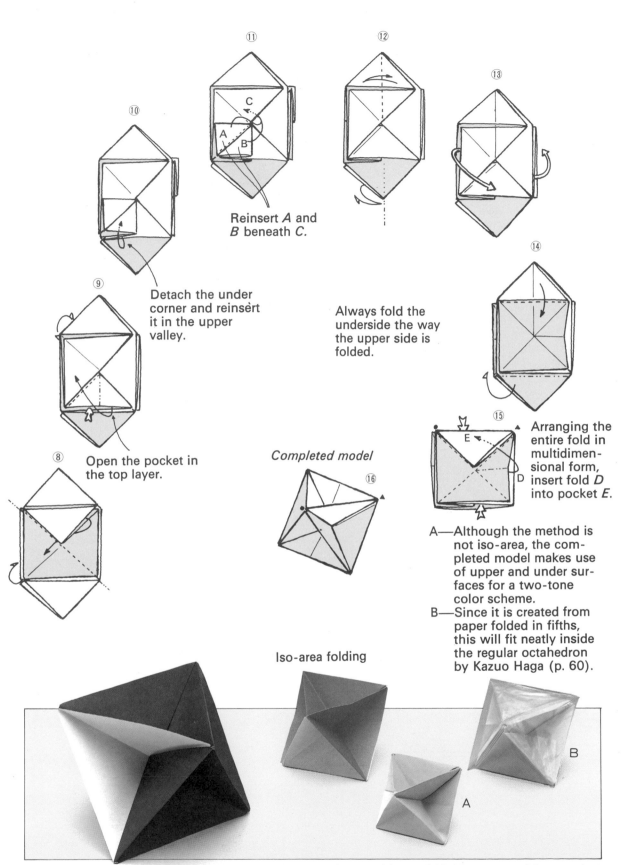

⑪

⑫

⑬

C

A B

Reinsert *A* and
B beneath *C*.

⑩

Always fold the
underside the way
the upper side is
folded.

⑨

Detach the under
corner and reinsèrt
it in the upper
valley.

⑭

⑧

Open the pocket in
the top layer.

Completed model

⑯

⑮

E

D

Arranging the
entire fold in
multidimen-
sional form,
insert fold *D*
into pocket *E*.

A—Although the method is
not iso-area, the com-
pleted model makes use
of upper and under sur-
faces for a two-tone
color scheme.
B—Since it is created from
paper folded in fifths,
this will fit neatly inside
the regular octahedron
by Kazuo Haga (p. 60).

Iso-area folding

B

A

Two-sheet assembly

(All of these Maekawa models were folded from paper of the same size.)

Dodecahedron Unit

Jun Maekawa

During the evolution of this book, Maekawa produced this truly remarkable, new dodeca-hedral unit. Those of you who did not manage to fold the Haga work on page 64 should try your hand at this one. Those of you who have tried the Haga dodecahedron will get an idea of the ease of single-sheet folding from working on this.

Each unit has two regular pentagonal faces. Thus it is easy to produce a dodecahedron from six of these units, each made from a single sheet of paper. Of course, all the units may be of one color. But it is more interesting to combine three colors.

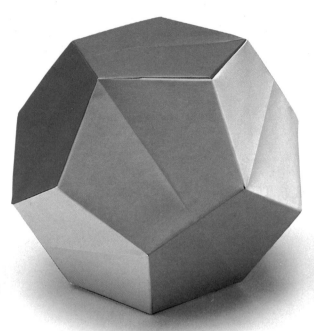

The dodecahedral unit in the photograph uses three colors.

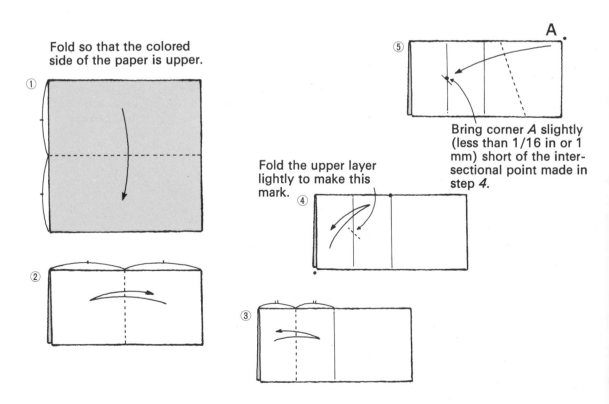

Fold so that the colored side of the paper is upper.

Fold the upper layer lightly to make this mark.

Bring corner *A* slightly (less than 1/16 in or 1 mm) short of the inter-sectional point made in step *4*.

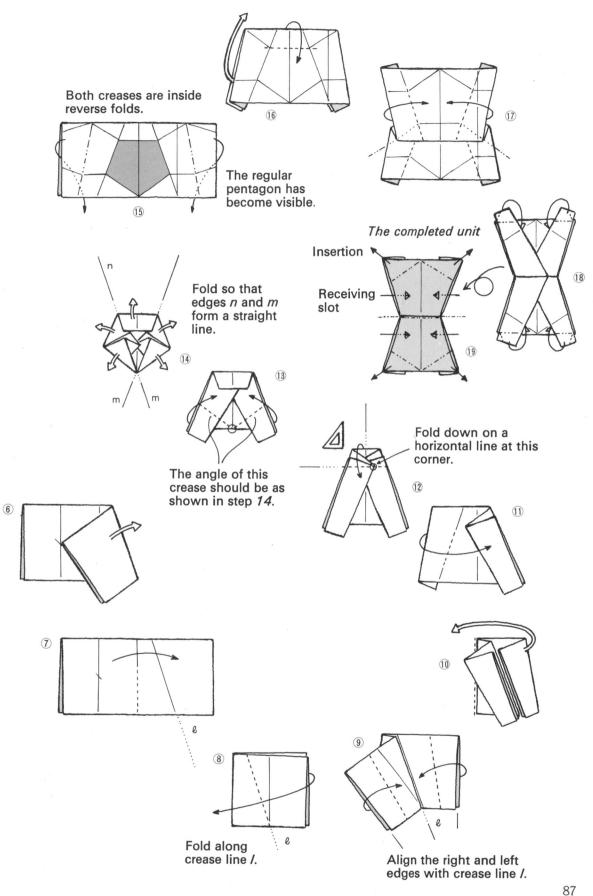

Both creases are inside reverse folds.

The regular pentagon has become visible.

⑮

⑯

⑰

The completed unit

Insertion

Receiving slot

⑱

⑲

n

Fold so that edges *n* and *m* form a straight line.

⑭

m   m

⑬

The angle of this crease should be as shown in step *14*.

Fold down on a horizontal line at this corner.

⑫

⑪

⑥

⑩

⑦

ℓ

⑧

Fold along crease line *l*.

ℓ

⑨

ℓ

Align the right and left edges with crease line *l*.

Octahedron Folded in the Iso-area Way

Toshikazu Kawasaki

This example shows how the iso-area folding method works the same even with nonsquare paper.

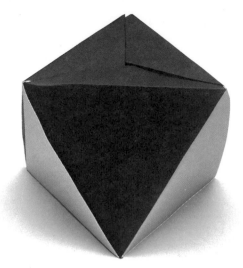

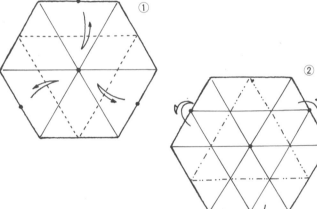

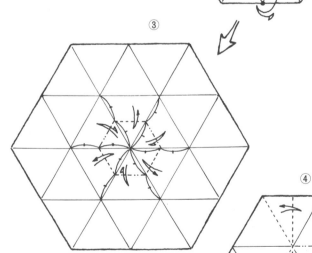

Explanation for the rest of the folding are not given here. Using the new technique, which by now you should have mastered, continue after step *5* to produce this familiar form.

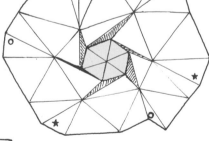

Assemble the three ○ marks on the upper surface and the three ★ marks on the under surface.

The small, regular hexagon, shown in red, is the central plate.

Regular-hexagonal Coaster

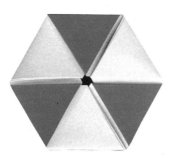

Pinwheel

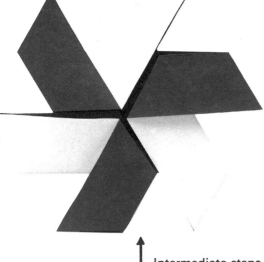

Intermediate steps not shown.

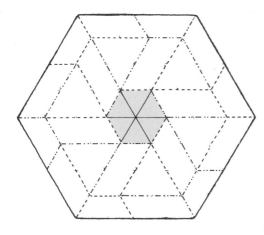

For review, fold the shapes shown above.

Intermediate steps not shown.

Preparing Regular-hexagonal Paper

①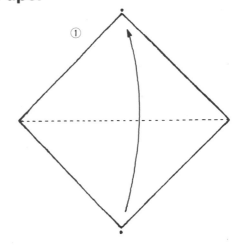

②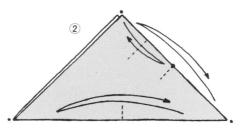

③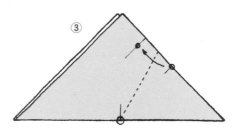

④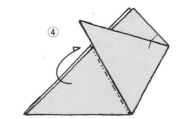

⑤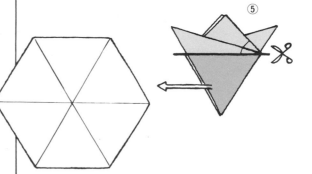

Ptarmigan— Icosahedron

Kohji and Mitsue Fushimi

The final work in this chapter is a masterpiece demonstrating a fusion of rationality and lyricism. In addition, it deserves special commemoration as representing the origami enthusiasm of the already internationally known Kohji Fushimi and his wife Mitsue.

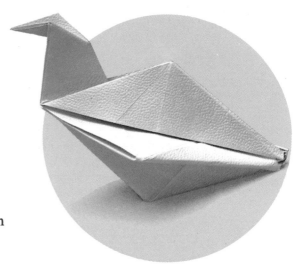

This captivating ptarmigan, prepared from regular-hexagonal paper on the preceding page, may be inflated in a way that, as if by magic, converts it into a regular icosahedron. It is best to make it of a large piece of thin, strong paper.

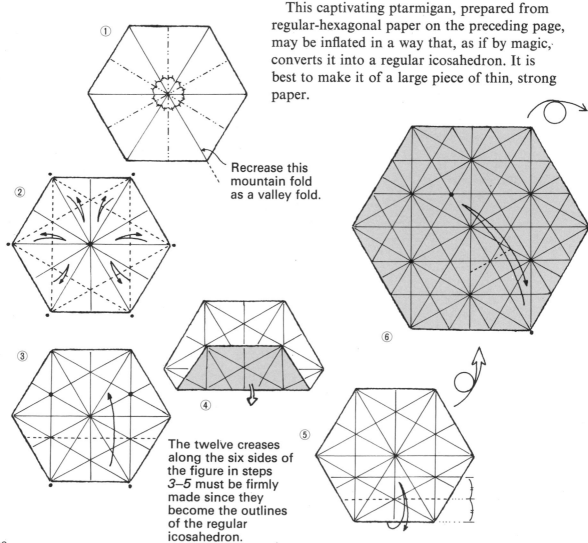

Recrease this mountain fold as a valley fold.

The twelve creases along the six sides of the figure in steps 3–5 must be firmly made since they become the outlines of the regular icosahedron.

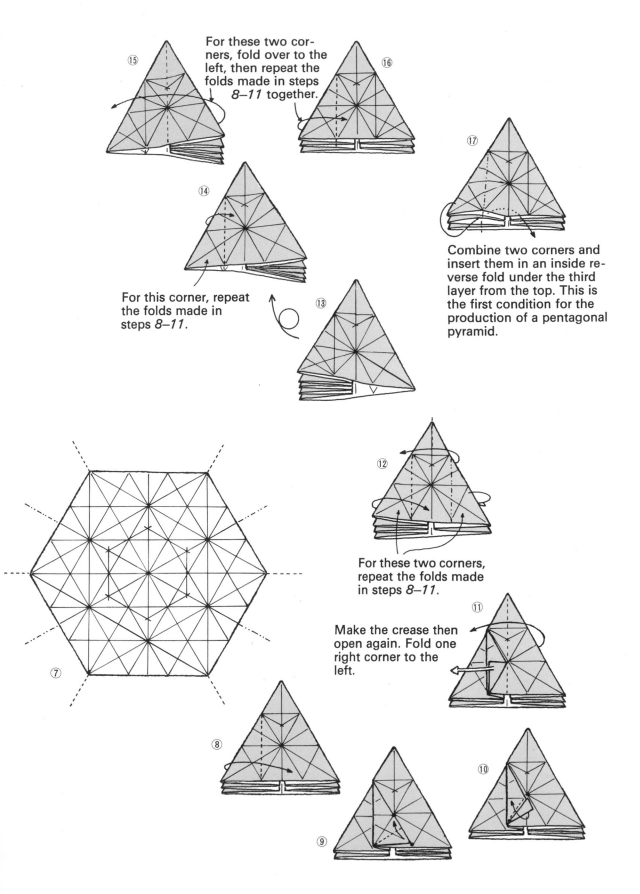

For these two corners, fold over to the left, then repeat the folds made in steps *8–11* together.

⑮

⑯

⑰

Combine two corners and insert them in an inside reverse fold under the third layer from the top. This is the first condition for the production of a pentagonal pyramid.

⑭

For this corner, repeat the folds made in steps *8–11*.

⑬

⑦

⑫

For these two corners, repeat the folds made in steps *8–11*.

⑪

Make the crease then open again. Fold one right corner to the left.

⑧

⑩

⑨

91

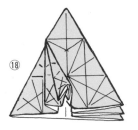

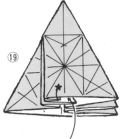

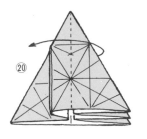

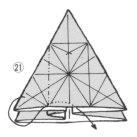

⑱ ⑲ ⑳ ㉑

Fold this corner inward on premade creases. Simultaneously fold the double triangular corner marked ★

Now make an inside reverse fold with one corner only then repeat the foldings in steps *17–19*

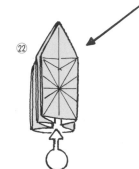

㉒

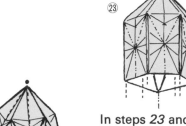

㉓

The completed pentagonal pyramid

In steps *23* and *24*, the internal triangular parts are oriented in the same direction.

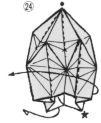

㉔

Though the process is difficult, in steps *24* and *25*, quickly arrange the form according to the creases in step *6*.

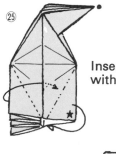

㉕

Insert the corner within the pleat.

Inside reverse fold

Insert the remaining three corners in the same way.

㉖

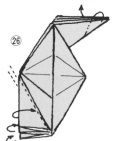

㉗

Completed ptarmigan

After the icosahedron has been completed, gently pushing the air out, return the fold to its ptarmigan shape.

Metamorphosis initiated.

Insert a straw in the hole in the figure and blow.

Chapter 2

Creases Have Messages to Make

Competing for the Fun of It

This book contains a collection of selected origami works on various themes. In the process of selection, some solutions to the problems inherent in those themes have had to be eliminated. Although this by no means implies superiority and inferiority in quality, a friendly, enjoyable spirit of competition among origamians is important for the stimulating effect it has on origami progress. In the sense that works introduced here represent a pinnacle in enthusiasm and effort, they are, as I hope the reader will realize, both tops in merit and topical in interest.

Vary the facial expressions.

Kitten

Toshikazu Kawasaki

The paper is folded into eighths simply for the sake of ease in working. A long, narrow piece of paper is essential.

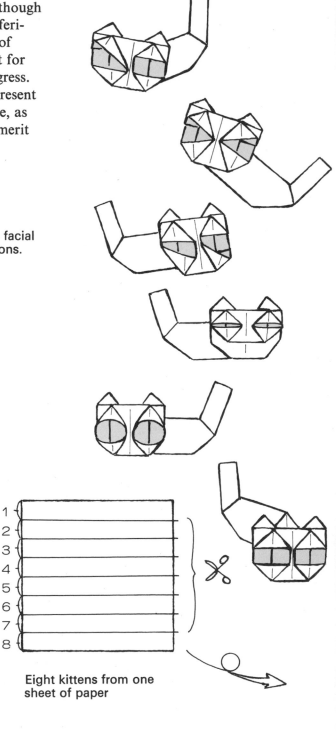

Eight kittens from one sheet of paper

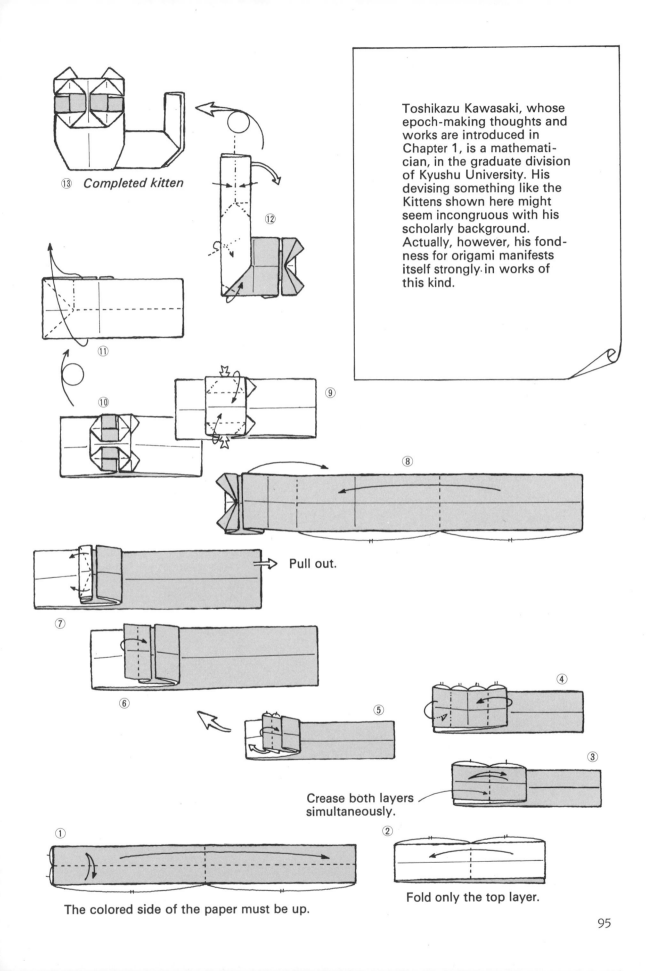

⑬ *Completed kitten*

Toshikazu Kawasaki, whose epoch-making thoughts and works are introduced in Chapter 1, is a mathematician, in the graduate division of Kyushu University. His devising something like the Kittens shown here might seem incongruous with his scholarly background. Actually, however, his fondness for origami manifests itself strongly in works of this kind.

⑪

⑫

⑩

⑨

⑧

Pull out.

⑦

⑥

⑤

④

Crease both layers simultaneously.

③

①

② Fold only the top layer.

The colored side of the paper must be up.

New Developments on Basic Patterns

The traditional basic patterns, like the bird base and frog base shown on the right, have generally been used as they are in various works, whose nature is related to the number of pointed segments available in each of the bases. Gradually, however, as their number increased, folds of this kind tended to become stereotyped. The need to break new ground stimulated origamians to develop different basic forms and in this way to make contributions to the progress of origami as a whole.

In addition, however, other new principles (like the Haga theorem) and techniques resulted in various processes that, transcending consideration of the number of pointed segments available, seem almost magical. The works shown in the photographs below are clearly produced on the basis of the processes involved in making the bird base, though they cannot be connected with numbers of pointed segments and therefore represent novel developments on basic patterns.

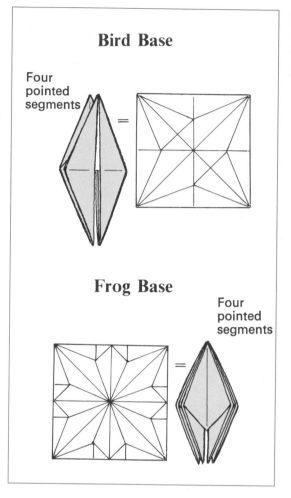

Bird Base

Four pointed segments

Frog Base

Four pointed segments

Goose by John Montroll (p. 98)

Snail Shell by Toshikazu Kawasaki (p. 140)

From the Bird Base
As unbelievable as it seems, this was made from one bird base with no cutting at all.

Kangaroo by Peter Engel
(p. 106)

Other new developments appear in the following pages.

Lidded Sea-snail Shell by Toshikazu Kawasaki (Variation of the work shown on p. 140)

Divided *Masu* Measuring Box by Jun Maekawa

As is explained in Chapter 1, this measuring box is made from the bird base.

Goose

John Montroll

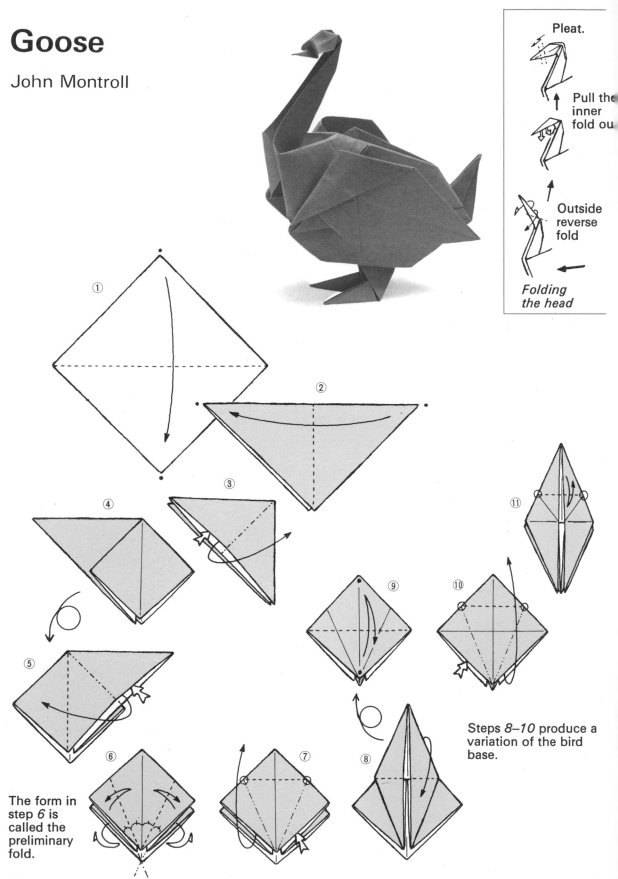

Pleat.

Pull the inner fold ou

Outside reverse fold

Folding the head

The form in step *6* is called the preliminary fold.

Steps *8–10* produce a variation of the bird base.

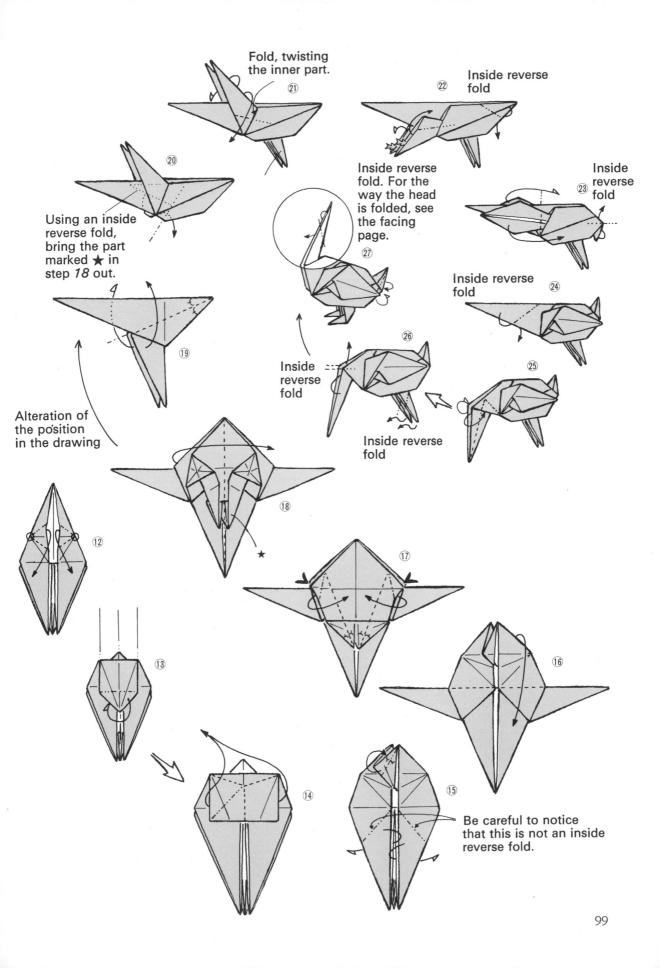

Fold, twisting
the inner part.
㉑

㉒ Inside reverse
fold

Inside reverse
fold. For the
way the head
is folded, see
the facing
page.
㉗

Inside
reverse
㉓ fold

㉔ Inside reverse
fold

Inside
reverse
fold

Inside reverse
fold

㉕

㉖

Using an inside
reverse fold,
bring the part
marked ★ in
step 18 out.

㉚

⑲

Alteration of
the position
in the drawing

⑫

⑱

★

⑰

⑬

⑯

⑭

⑮

Be careful to notice
that this is not an inside
reverse fold.

99

Pelican

John Montroll

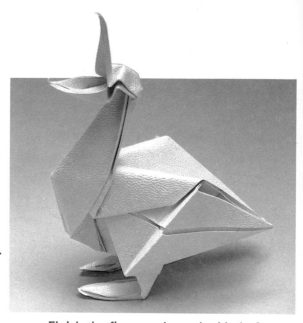

One of the most promising members of the
New York Origami Center, John Montroll
has been publishing outstanding works since
the age of nine. Like Toshikazu Kawasaki, he is
a mathematician—at the University of Michigan.
He and Peter Engel, another promising young
American origamian, whose work is introduced
later, are good friends.

Finish the figure to have the kind of
full, richly dimensional appearance
seen in the photograph.

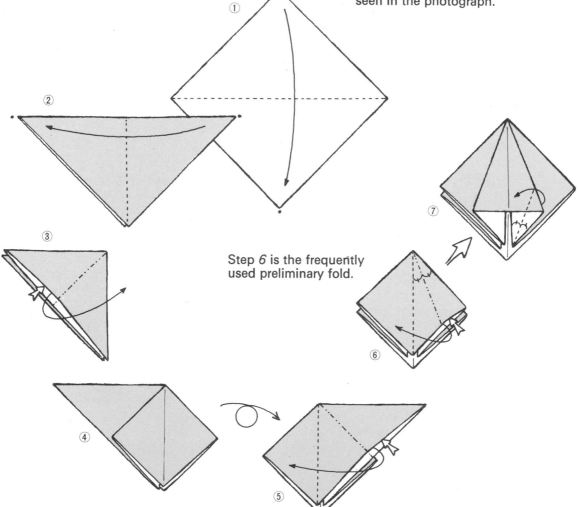

Step *6* is the frequently
used preliminary fold.

100

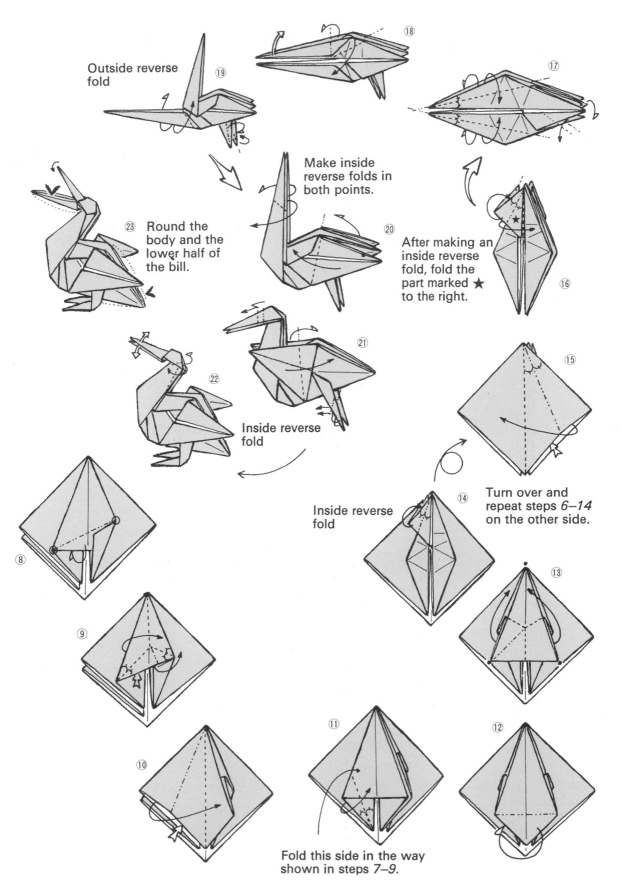

Outside reverse fold

Make inside reverse folds in both points.

After making an inside reverse fold, fold the part marked ★ to the right.

Round the body and the lower half of the bill.

Inside reverse fold

Inside reverse fold

Turn over and repeat steps *6–14* on the other side.

Fold this side in the way shown in steps *7–9*.

⑧ ⑨ ⑩ ⑪ ⑫ ⑬ ⑭ ⑮ ⑯ ⑰ ⑱ ⑲ ⑳ ㉑ ㉒ ㉓

101

Clapper Rail

Jun Maekawa

The rails, small wading birds
resembling cranes, have short
wings and tail, long toes, and a
harsh cry.

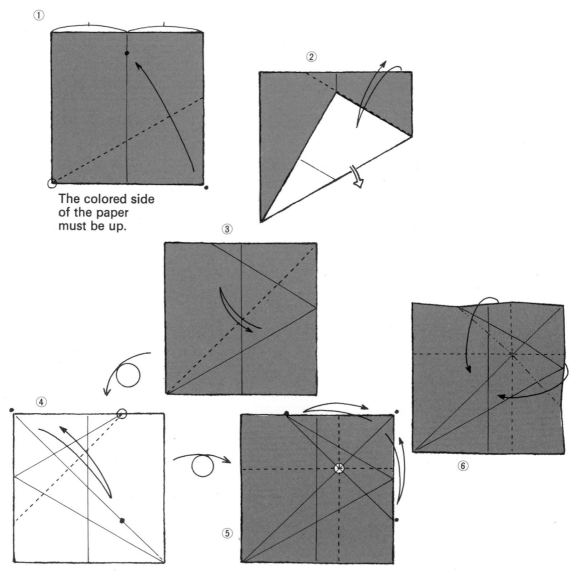

①

The colored side
of the paper
must be up.

②

③

④

⑤

⑥

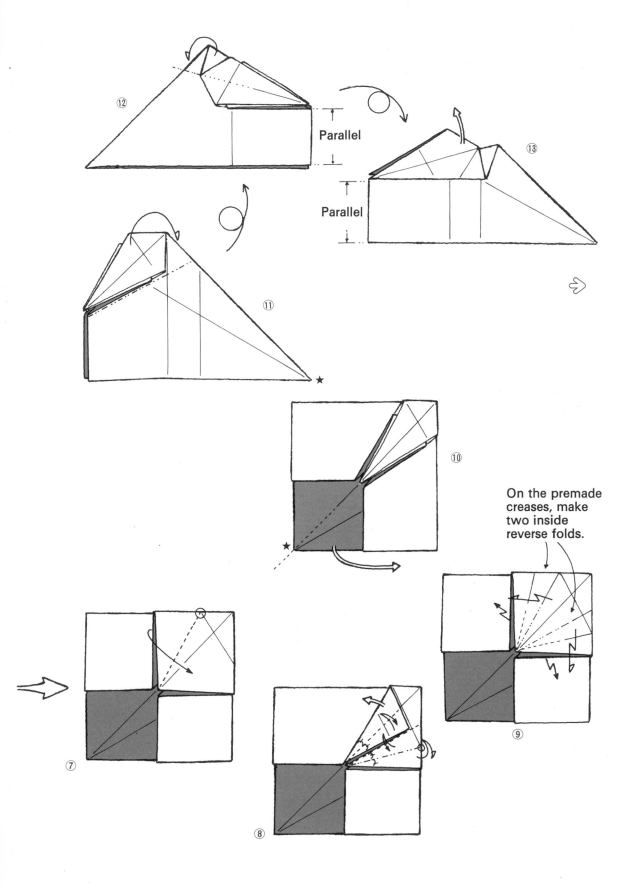

Parallel

Parallel

On the premade
creates, make
two inside
reverse folds.

⑦ ⑧ ⑨ ⑩ ⑪ ⑫ ⑬

103

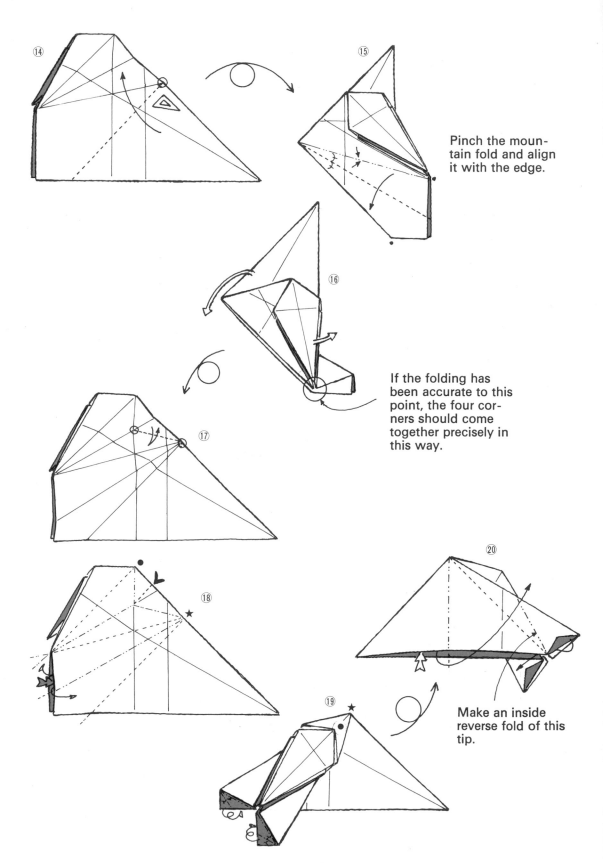

Pinch the mountain fold and align it with the edge.

If the folding has been accurate to this point, the four corners should come together precisely in this way.

Make an inside reverse fold of this tip.

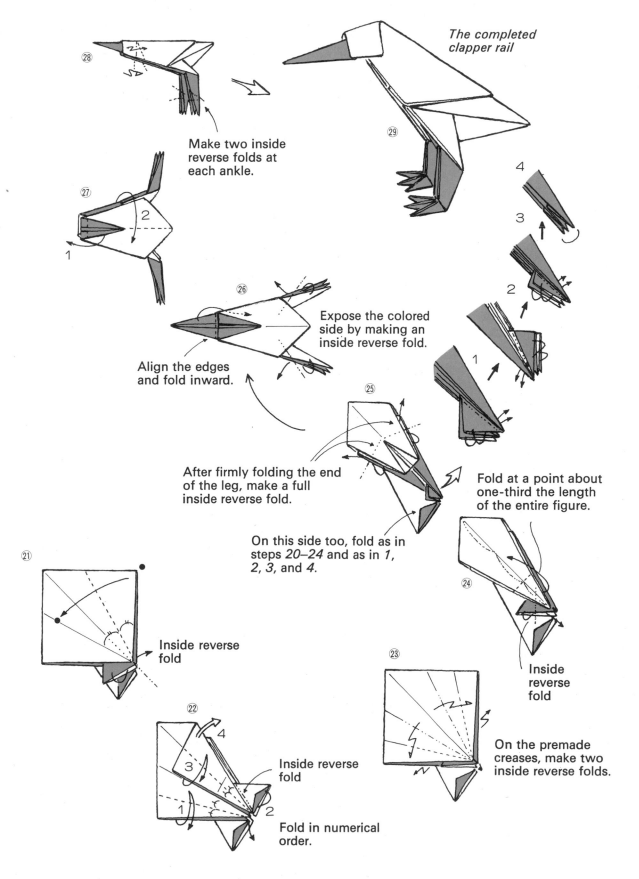

㉘ Make two inside reverse folds at each ankle.

㉙ *The completed clapper rail*

4

3

2

1

㉗

2

1

㉖ Expose the colored side by making an inside reverse fold.

Align the edges and fold inward.

㉕

After firmly folding the end of the leg, make a full inside reverse fold.

On this side too, fold as in steps *20–24* and as in *1, 2, 3,* and *4.*

Fold at a point about one-third the length of the entire figure.

㉔

Inside reverse fold

㉑

Inside reverse fold

㉓

On the premade creases, make two inside reverse folds.

㉒

4

3

2

1

Inside reverse fold

Fold in numerical order.

Kangaroo

Peter Engel

The mother kangaroo and the baby
thrusting its head out of the pouch in
her belly are folded from the same
piece of paper.

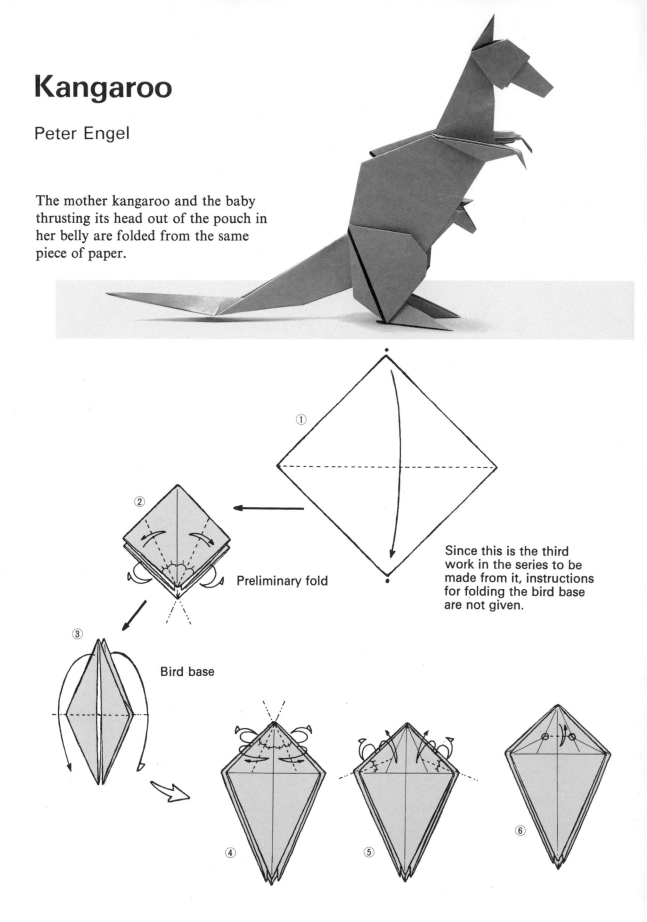

①

② Preliminary fold

Since this is the third
work in the series to be
made from it, instructions
for folding the bird base
are not given.

③ Bird base

④

⑤

⑥

106

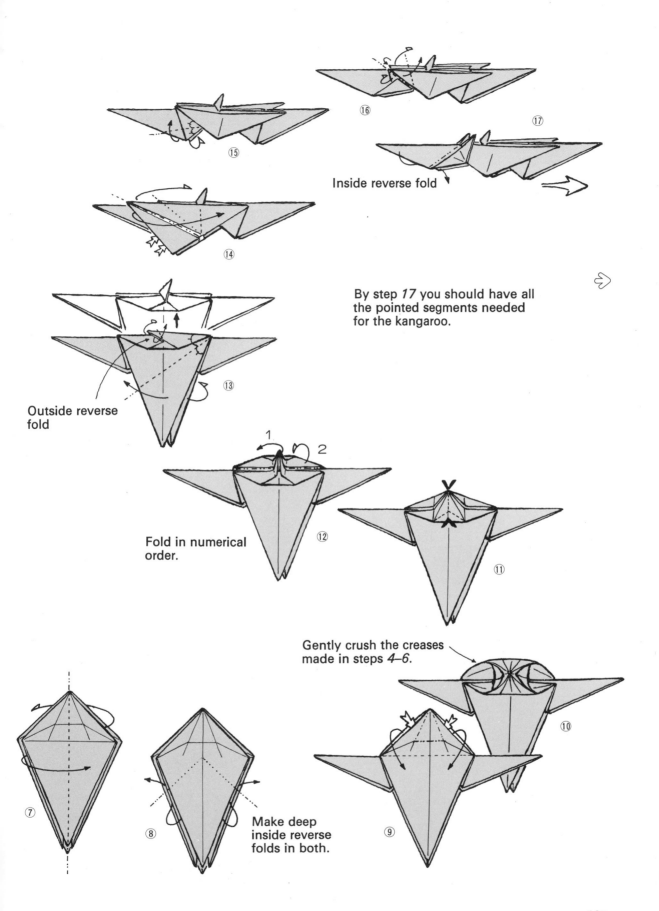

⑯

⑰

Inside reverse fold ↓

By step *17* you should have all
the pointed segments needed
for the kangaroo.

⑮

⑭

Outside reverse
fold

⑬

1   2

Fold in numerical
order.

⑫

⑪

Gently crush the creases
made in steps *4–6*.

⑩

⑦

⑧

Make deep
inside reverse
folds in both.

⑨

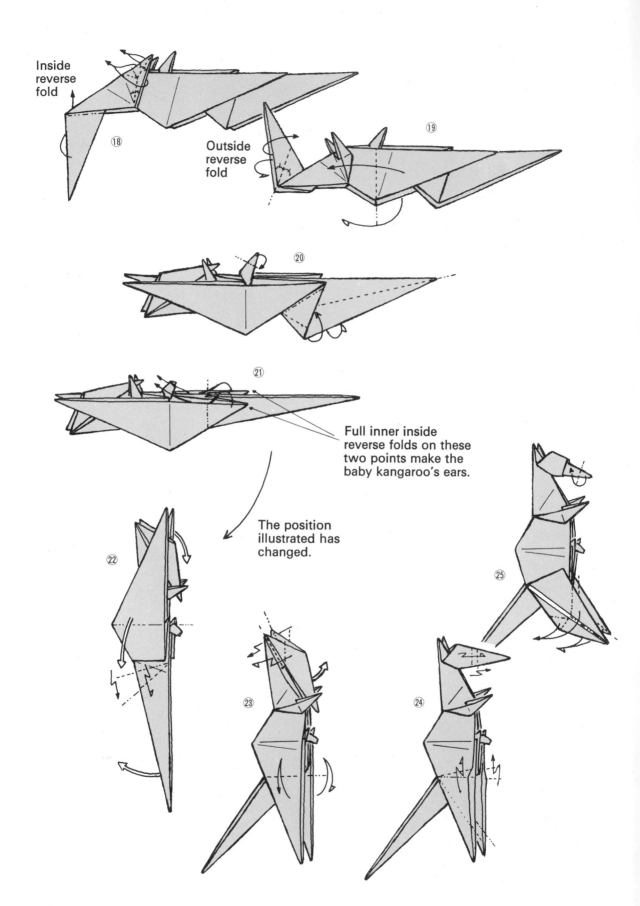

Inside reverse fold

Outside reverse fold

Full inner inside reverse folds on these two points make the baby kangaroo's ears.

The position illustrated has changed.

A graduate of Harvard, Peter Engel is, as this work makes clear, a top-class origami artist. In addition, he very quickly assimilates new knowledge and is certain to be an outstanding leader contributing much to the development of the origami of the future.

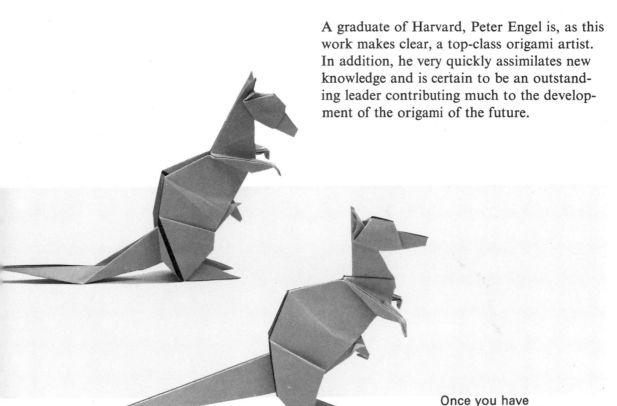

Once you have mastered the folding method, make several kangaroos in different postures.

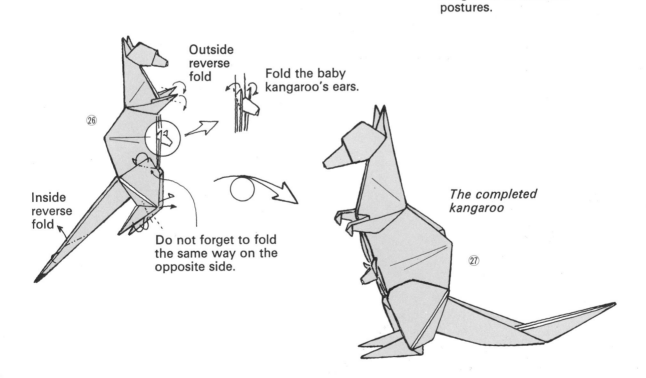

Outside reverse fold

Fold the baby kangaroo's ears.

㉖

Inside reverse fold

Do not forget to fold the same way on the opposite side.

The completed kangaroo

㉗

109

Giraffe

Peter Engel

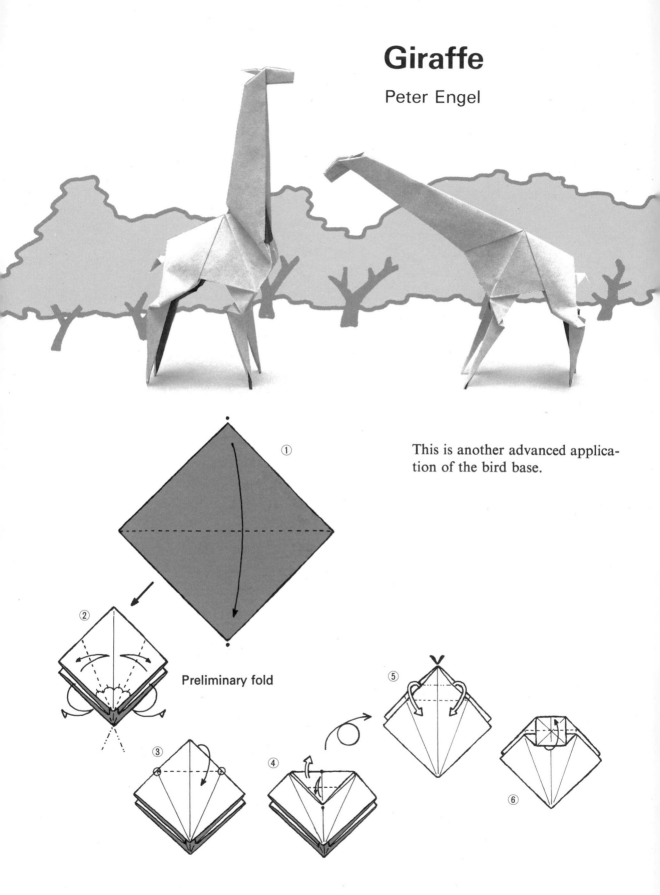

①

This is another advanced application of the bird base.

② Preliminary fold

③

④

⑤

⑥

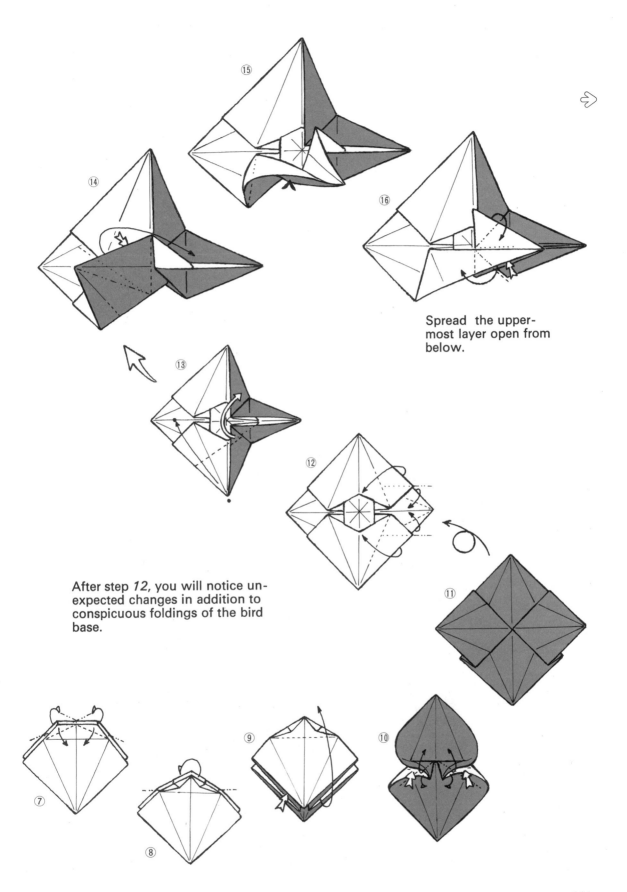

⑮

⑭

⑯

Spread the upper-
most layer open from
below.

⑬

⑫

After step *12*, you will notice unexpected changes in addition to
conspicuous foldings of the bird
base.

⑪

⑦

⑧

⑨

⑩

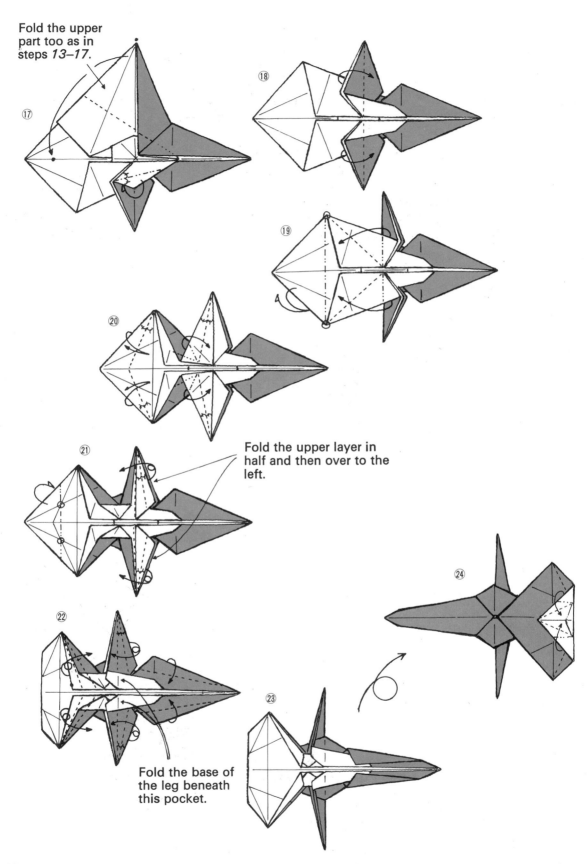

Fold the upper part too as in steps *13–17*.

Fold the upper layer in half and then over to the left.

Fold the base of the leg beneath this pocket.

112

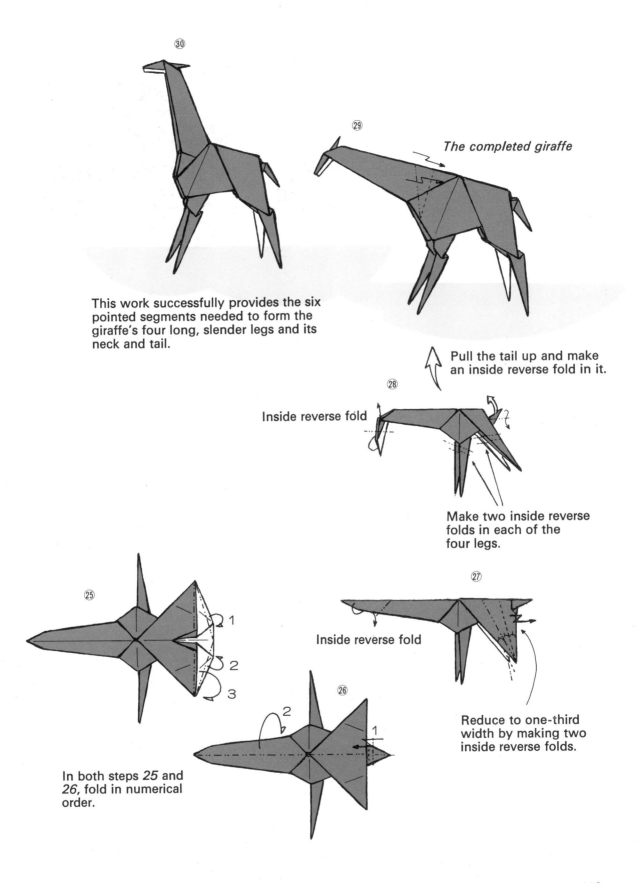

㉚

㉙

The completed giraffe

This work successfully provides the six pointed segments needed to form the giraffe's four long, slender legs and its neck and tail.

Pull the tail up and make an inside reverse fold in it.

㉘

Inside reverse fold

Make two inside reverse folds in each of the four legs.

㉗

Inside reverse fold

Reduce to one-third width by making two inside reverse folds.

㉕

1

2

3

㉖

2

1

In both steps *25* and *26*, fold in numerical order.

Malay Tapir

Jun Maekawa

Use paper that is black on one
side and white on the other.

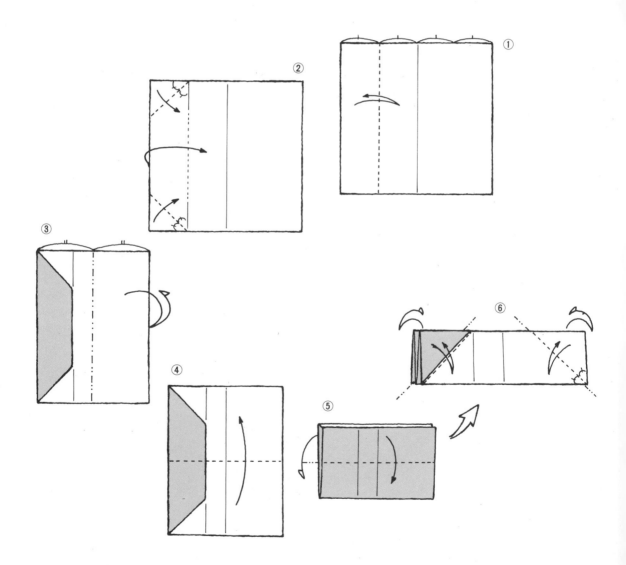

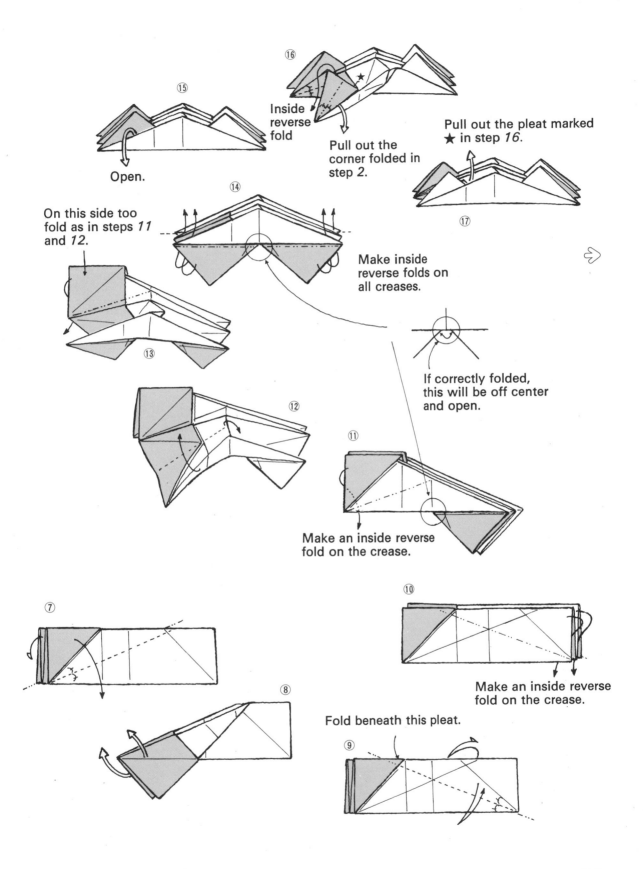

⑯

Inside
reverse
fold

Pull out the
corner folded in
step *2*.

Pull out the pleat marked
★ in step *16*.

⑮

Open.

On this side too
fold as in steps *11*
and *12*.

⑭

Make inside
reverse folds on
all creases.

⑰

⑬

If correctly folded,
this will be off center
and open.

⑫

⑪

Make an inside reverse
fold on the crease.

⑦

⑩

Make an inside reverse
fold on the crease.

Fold beneath this pleat.

⑧

⑨

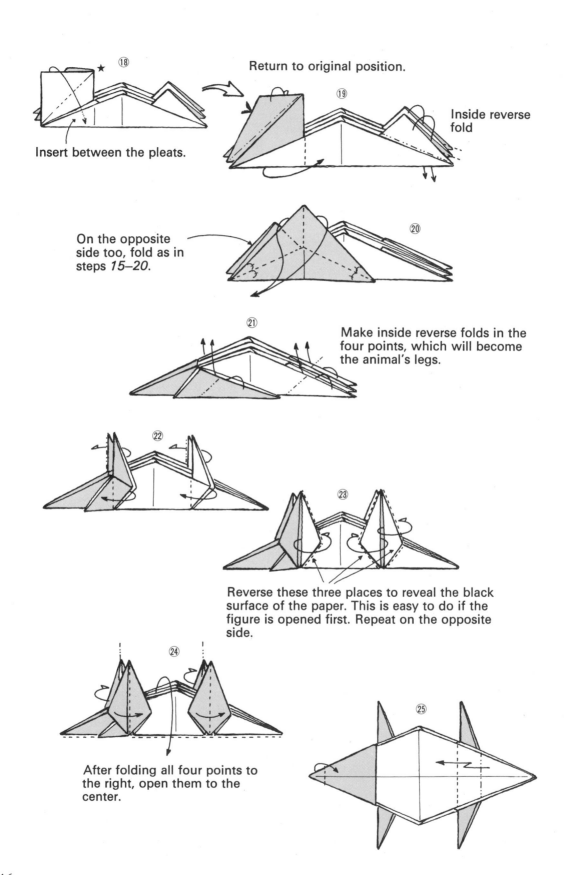

⑱

Insert between the pleats.

Return to original position.

⑲

Inside reverse fold

On the opposite side too, fold as in steps *15–20*.

⑳

㉑

Make inside reverse folds in the four points, which will become the animal's legs.

㉒

㉓

Reverse these three places to reveal the black surface of the paper. This is easy to do if the figure is opened first. Repeat on the opposite side.

㉔

After folding all four points to the right, open them to the center.

㉕

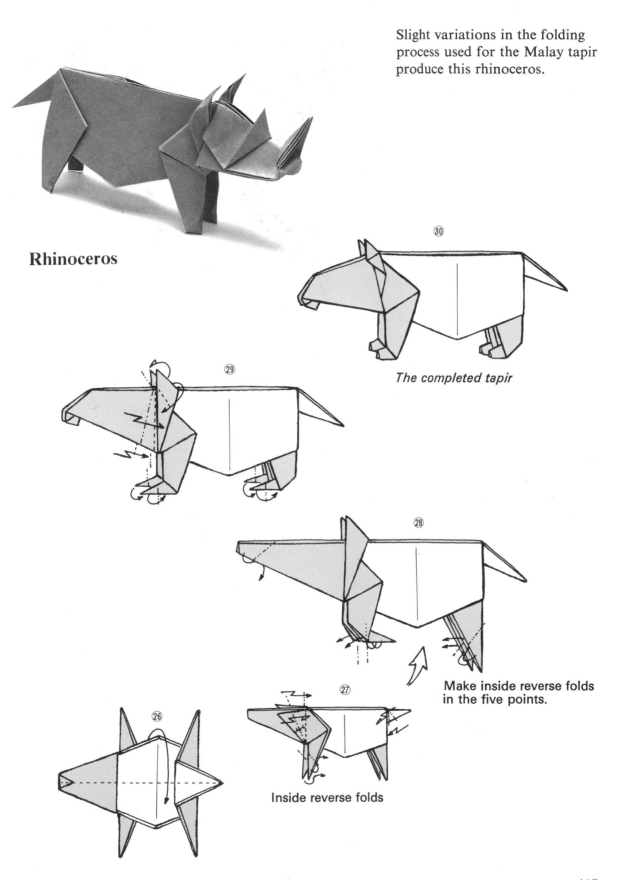

Slight variations in the folding process used for the Malay tapir produce this rhinoceros.

Rhinoceros

㉚

The completed tapir

㉙

㉘

Make inside reverse folds in the five points.

㉗

Inside reverse folds

㉖

Horse

David Brill

This fold skillfully provides the pointed segments needed to produce the horse's four legs, neck, and tail from a piece of equilateral-triangular paper, which, of course, has one less corner than the usual square paper. The delicacy of the finishing makes it advisable to use a large piece of paper.

The illustration shows how to make an equilateral triangle of maximum area from a given square (see p. 62).

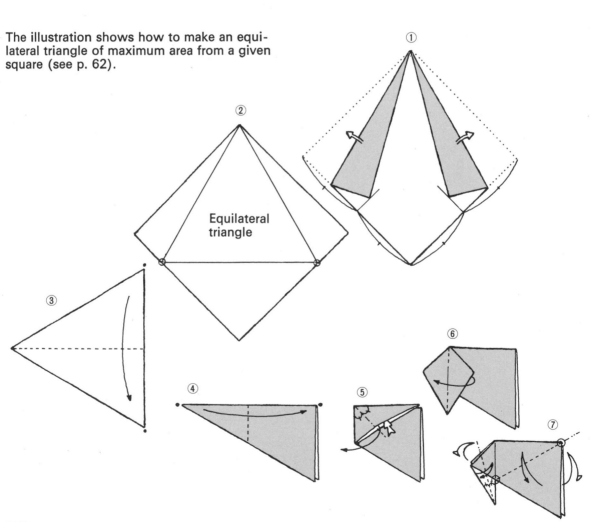

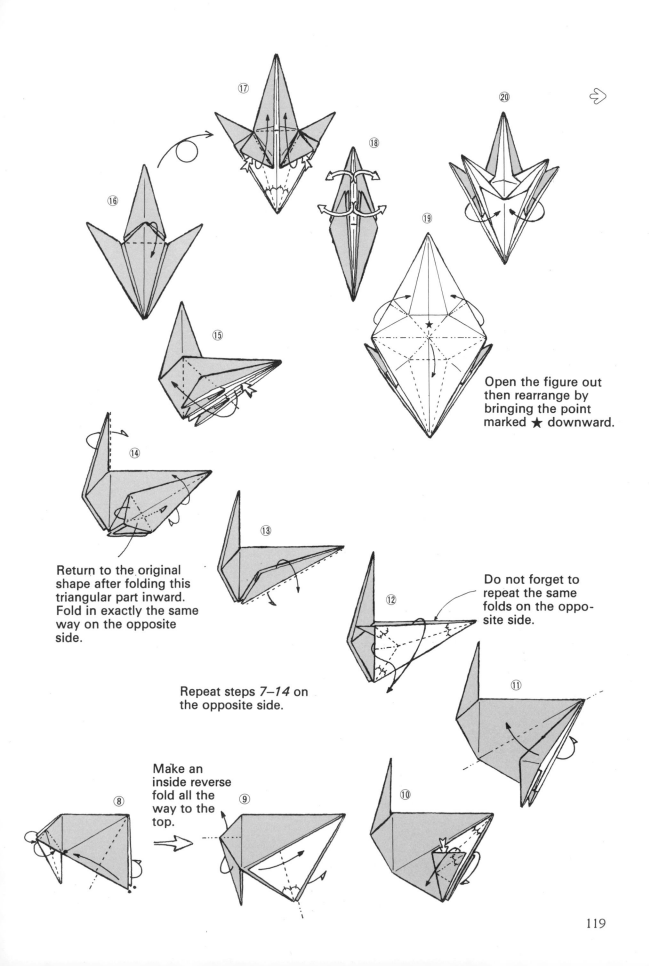

Open the figure out then rearrange by bringing the point marked ★ downward.

Return to the original shape after folding this triangular part inward. Fold in exactly the same way on the opposite side.

Do not forget to repeat the same folds on the opposite side.

Repeat steps 7–14 on the opposite side.

Make an inside reverse fold all the way to the top.

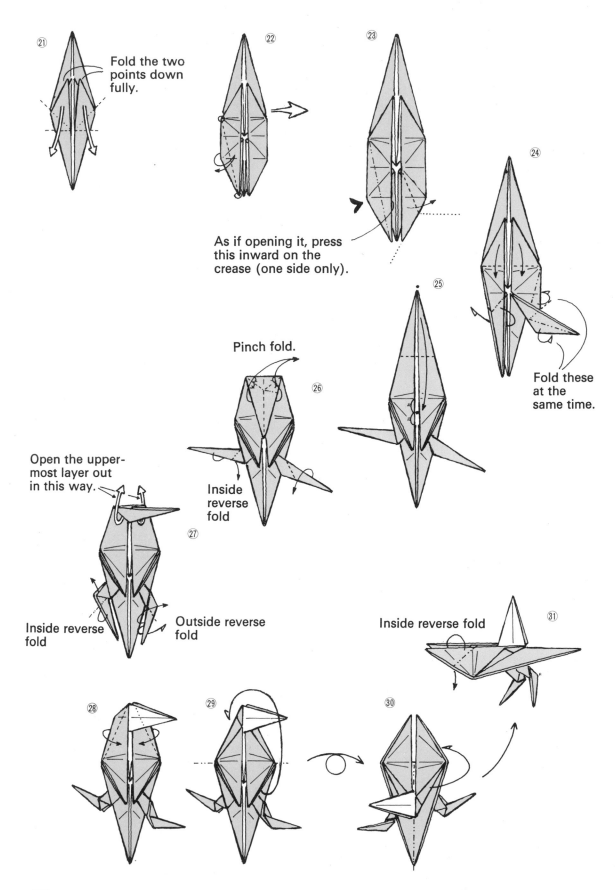

㉑ Fold the two points down fully.

㉒

㉓ As if opening it, press this inward on the crease (one side only).

㉔

㉕ Fold these at the same time.

Pinch fold.

㉖

Inside reverse fold

Open the uppermost layer out in this way.

㉗

Inside reverse fold

Outside reverse fold

Inside reverse fold

㉛

㉘

㉙

㉚

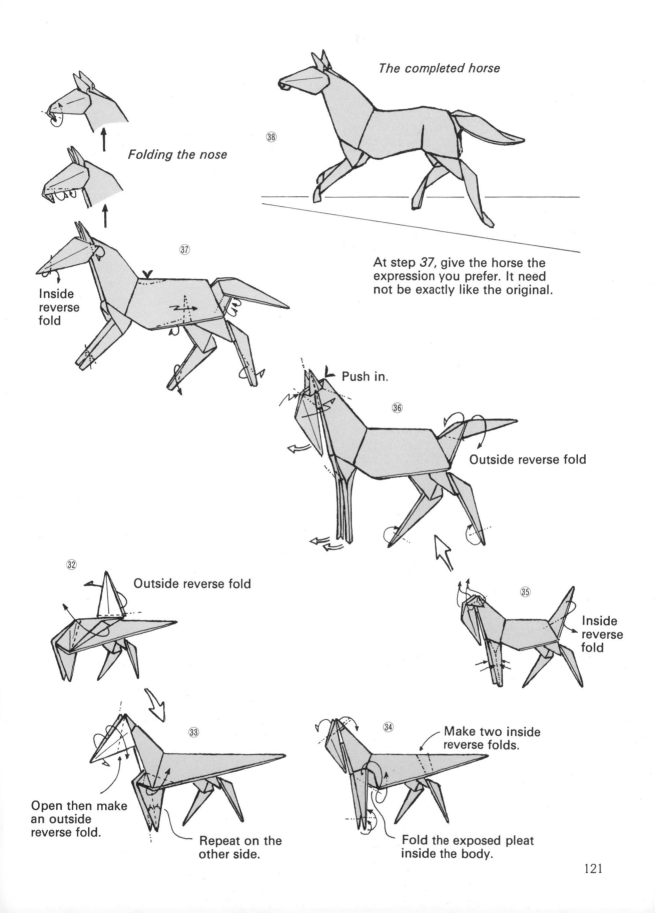

Folding the nose

The completed horse

③⑧

Inside reverse fold

③⑦

At step *37*, give the horse the expression you prefer. It need not be exactly like the original.

Push in.

③⑥

Outside reverse fold

③②

Outside reverse fold

③⑤

Inside reverse fold

③③

Open then make an outside reverse fold.

Repeat on the other side.

③④

Make two inside reverse folds.

Fold the exposed pleat inside the body.

121

Fox

Toshikazu Kawasaki

The fox in the photograph has been folded
from a piece of paper one-third as wide as
it is long. But, since the head and especially
the natural expression resulting from the
shadows created by the pleats in the
vicinity of the eyes are the most important
feature, it is a good idea to begin by
folding the head only from a piece of
square paper.

Fox head

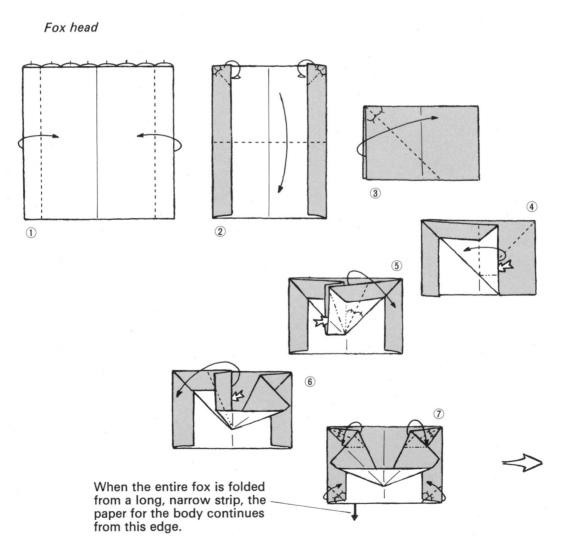

When the entire fox is folded
from a long, narrow strip, the
paper for the body continues
from this edge.

Fold as for the head up to step *10*.

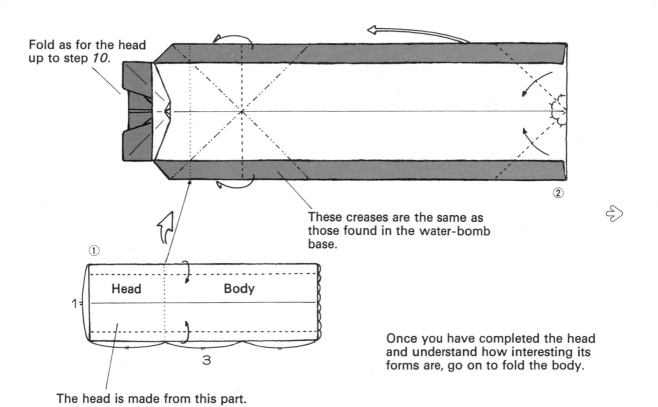

②

These creases are the same as those found in the water-bomb base.

①

| Head | Body |

1

3

The head is made from this part.

Once you have completed the head and understand how interesting its forms are, go on to fold the body.

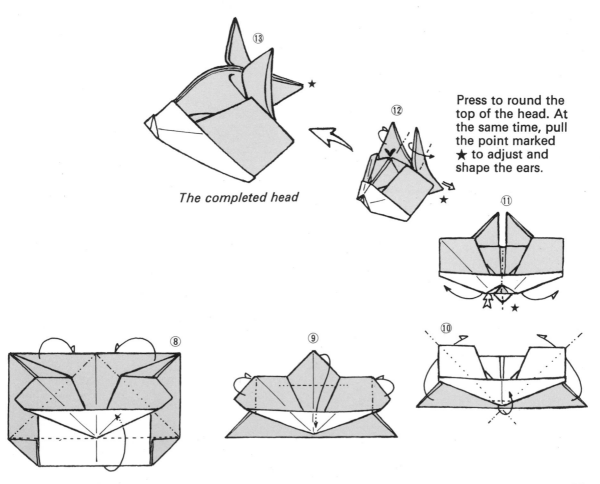

⑬

★

The completed head

Press to round the top of the head. At the same time, pull the point marked ★ to adjust and shape the ears.

⑫

★

★

⑪

★

⑧

⑨

⑩

123

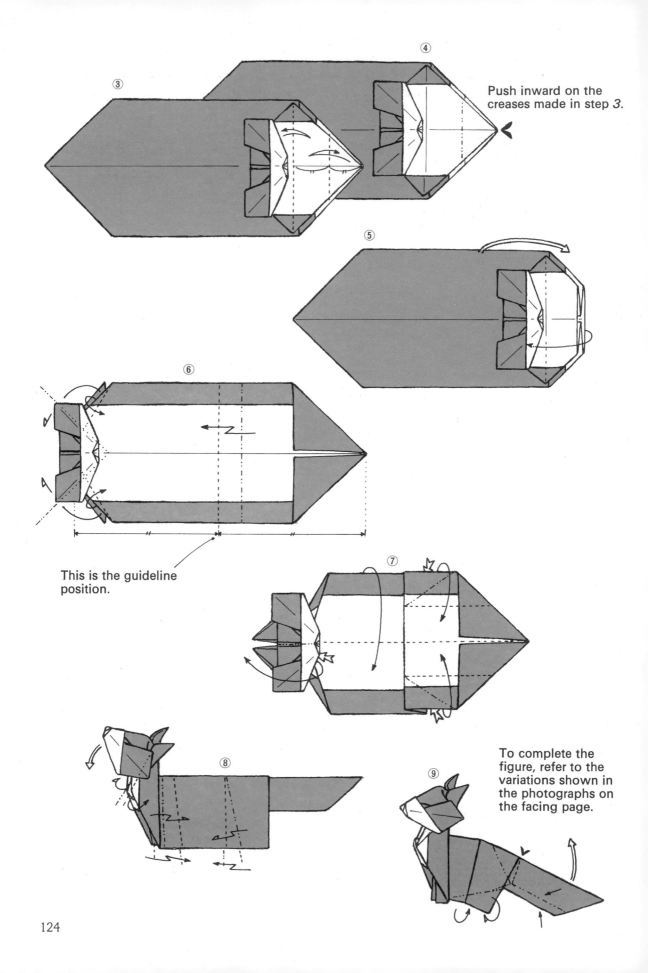

③

④ Push inward on the
creases made in step *3*.

⑤

⑥

This is the guideline
position.

⑦

⑧

⑨ To complete the
figure, refer to the
variations shown in
the photographs on
the facing page.

"The head is the form-building key point, and the expressions of the body are left to the folder." Following this advice from the designer of the fold, I produced the three variations shown below. Apply your ingenuity to devising still other versions.

Camellia, Bloom, and Branch

Toshie Takahama

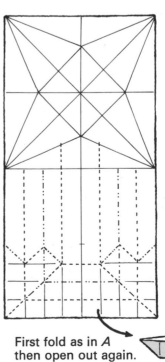

Yellow

Red

Green

Although using red, yellow, and green paper arranged as shown on the left produces a realistic effect, the camellia is attractively sophisticated folded all in white.

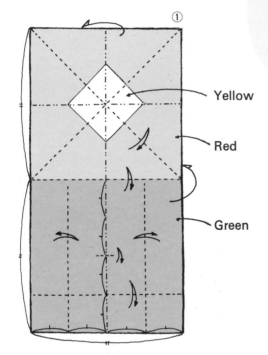

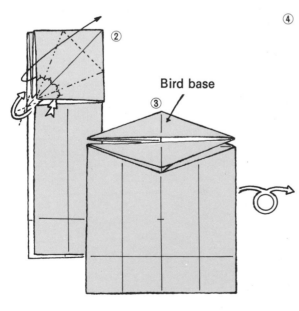

Bird base

First fold as in *A* then open out again.

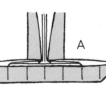

A

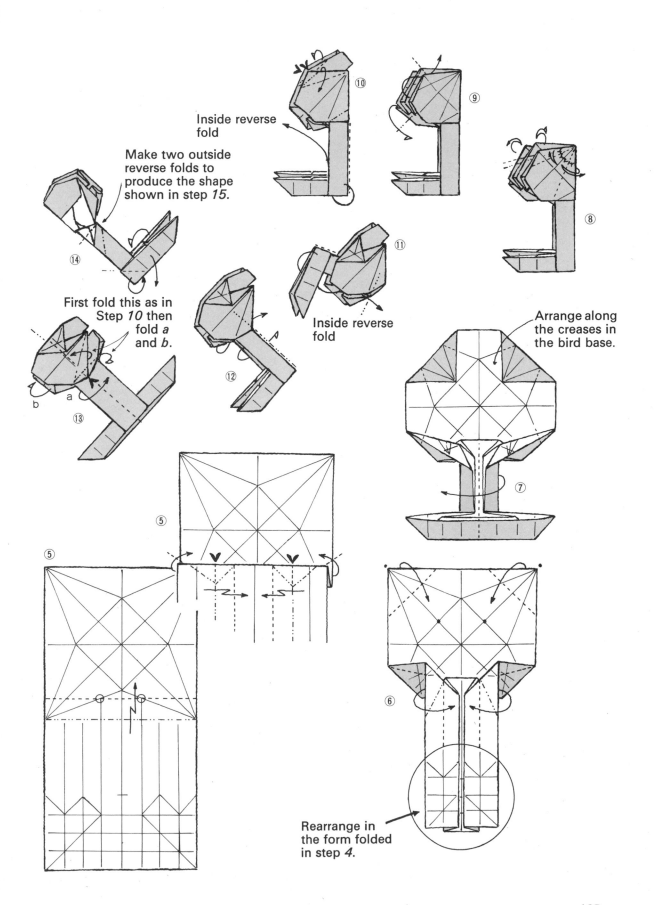

Inside reverse fold

Make two outside reverse folds to produce the shape shown in step *15*.

⑭

First fold this as in Step *10* then fold *a* and *b*.

b   a

⑬

⑩

⑨

⑧

⑪

Inside reverse fold

⑫

Arrange along the creases in the bird base.

⑦

⑤

⑤

⑥

Rearrange in the form folded in step *4*.

127

Rose

Toshikazu Kawasaki

As the photograph makes plain, this work is so soft and curvilinear in appearance as to seem not to have been folded at all. Nonetheless, it has been folded in a perfectly ordinary way without forcing. In terms of technique belonging in the category Shuzo Fujimoto calls twist-folding, this handsome rose makes use of Toshikazu Kawasaki's distinctive ingenuity and good taste.

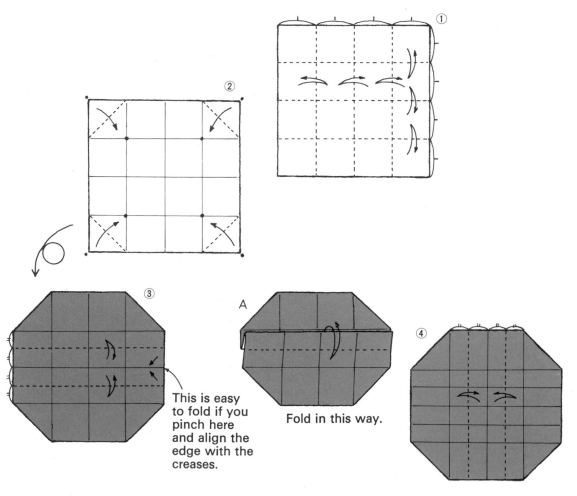

This is easy to fold if you pinch here and align the edge with the creases.

Fold in this way.

At step *10*, gripping the diagonal lines while you curl the creases marked *l* naturally will open a hole in the center and result in the curvilinear form shown in step *11*.

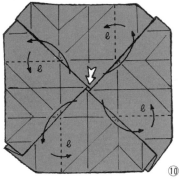

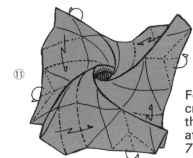
⑪

Fold on premade creases, mainly the ones produced at points *a* in step *7*.

From this point, no new creases are made until step *12* on the next page.

⑩

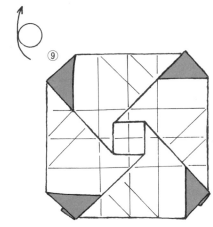
⑨

Twist as you fold to elevate the small square in the center.

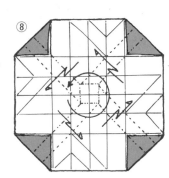
⑧

Steps *8* and *9* are the technique known as twist-folding.

Make creases in the manner shown in step *3-A*.

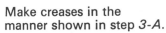

⑤
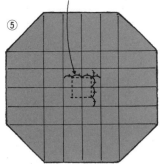

⑥

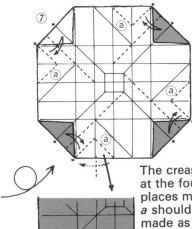
⑦

The creases at the four places marked *a* should be made as shown in the figure on the left.

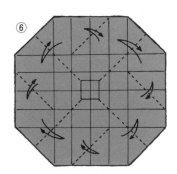

Inside reverse fold

129

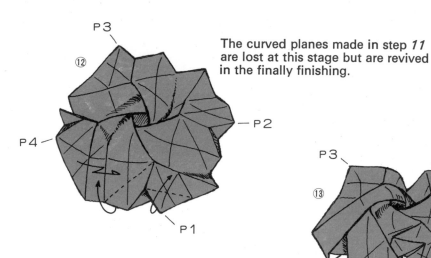

P3

⑫

P4

P2

P1

The curved planes made in step *11* are lost at this stage but are revived in the finally finishing.

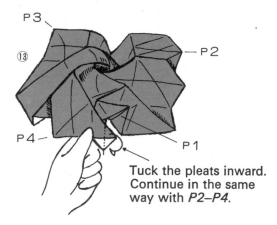

P3

⑬

P2

P4

P1

Tuck the pleats inward. Continue in the same way with *P2–P4*.

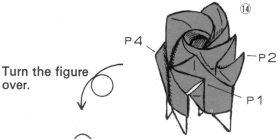

⑭

P4

P2

P1

Turn the figure over.

⑮

Without folding them, bend the four points inward.

⑯

The figure should be full and plump.

Curl the eight petals in an un-forced, natural way.

Mr. Kawasaki has contrived a variety of roses using this twist-fold technique. One of them is shown on the left. By making small adjustments at the final finishing stage it is possible to expresses roses in all stages of development, from bud to full bloom. Try your hand at making a large number of lovely roses.

Blossom and Leaves

Bud

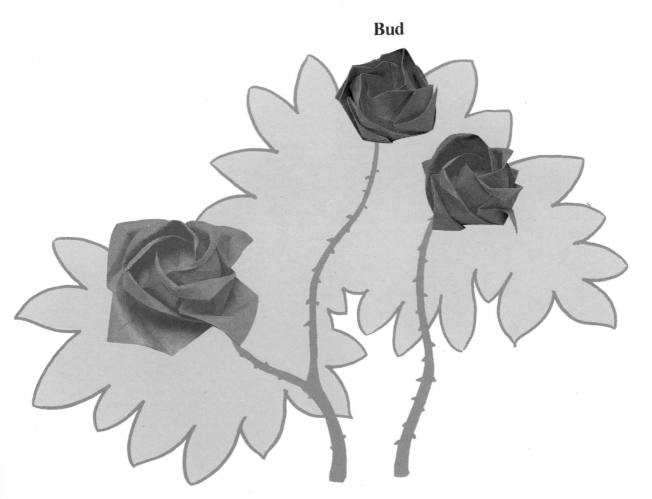

Three Vegetables

Toshikazu Kawasaki

Green Pepper

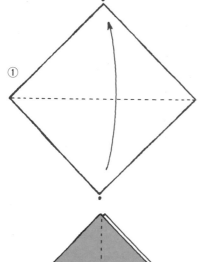

① ②

③

Green Pepper

④

⑤

Preliminary fold

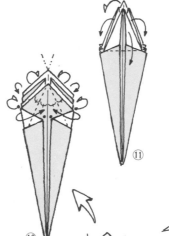

⑩

⑪

⑫

⑬

⑭

⑨ ⑧

Open out and turn
over to produce the
form seen in step *9*.

All three vegetables are
folded the same to
step *9*.

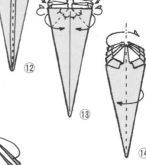

⑦

⑥

Fold these three
pockets the same
way.

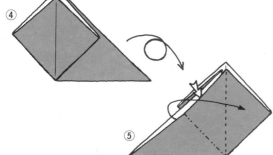

132

Eggplant

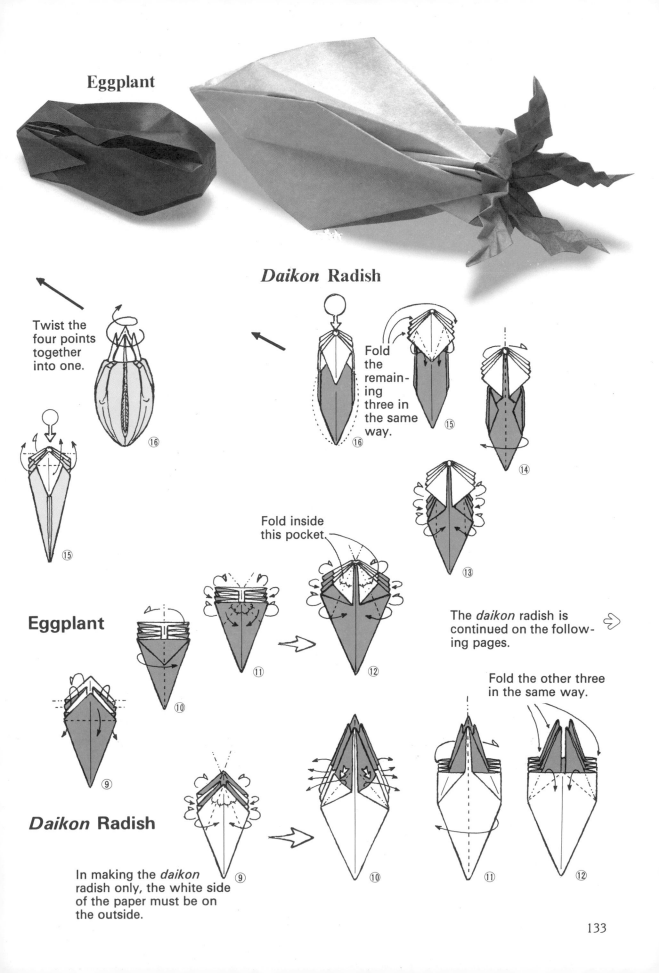

Daikon Radish

Twist the four points together into one.

⑯

⑮

Fold the remaining three in the same way.

⑯

⑮

⑭

Fold inside this pocket.

⑬

The *daikon* radish is continued on the following pages.

Eggplant

⑪

⑫

⑩

Fold the other three in the same way.

⑨

⑩

⑪

⑫

Daikon Radish

⑨

In making the *daikon* radish only, the white side of the paper must be on the outside.

133

Flower-cut Hard-boiled Egg

Toshikazu Kawasaki

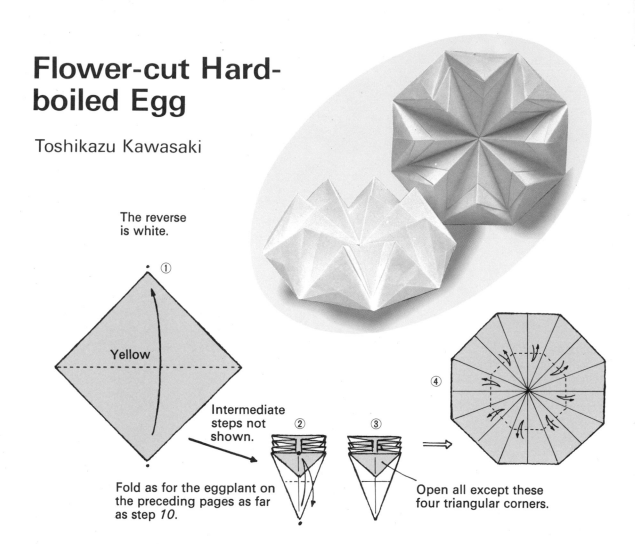

The reverse is white.

①

Yellow

Fold as for the eggplant on the preceding pages as far as step *10*.

Intermediate steps not shown.

② ③

Open all except these four triangular corners.

④

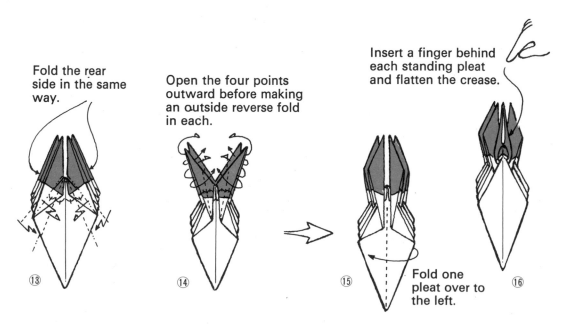

Fold the rear side in the same way.

Open the four points outward before making an outside reverse fold in each.

Insert a finger behind each standing pleat and flatten the crease.

⑬ ⑭ ⑮

Fold one pleat over to the left.

⑯

The idea of making an egg of folded paper is truly surprising and amusing. Each of the following series of superb works by Toshikazu Kawasaki too will reveal something surprising in model and folding method.

The completed flower-cut hard-boiled egg

⑩

Inflate the eight corners on the creases formed in step 7.

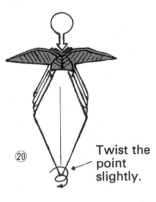

⑨

⑤

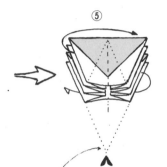

Adjust the shape by pushing this corner inward.

⑥

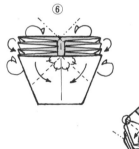

⑦

Crease the four internal corners in the same way.

⑧

Fold the remaining three points as in steps *15* and *16*.

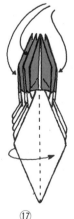

⑰

Make an inside reverse fold in each of the four points.

⑱

Make a series of inside reverse folds in the leaves to pleat them.

⑲

Examine the photograph of the completed *daikon* radish on page 133 and carefully adjust the shape of yours.

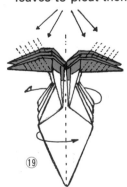

⑳

Twist the point slightly.

Pine Cone

Toshikazu Kawasaki

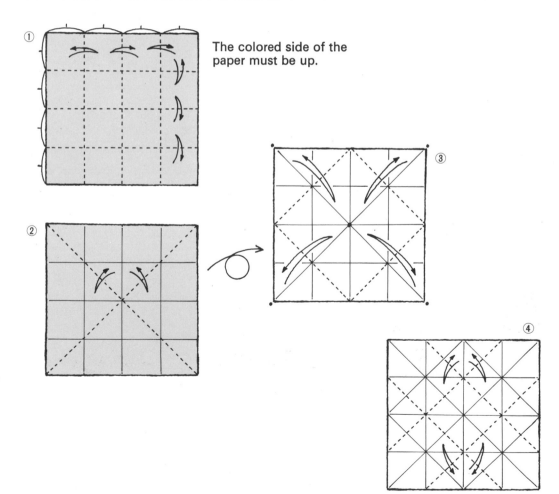

The colored side of the
paper must be up.

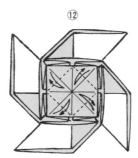

⑫

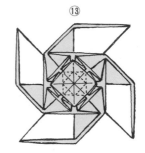

⑬

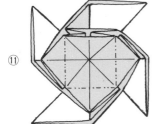

⑪

Repeat the series of folds in steps *8–11* three times.

Fold the remaining three corners as in steps *9* and *10*.

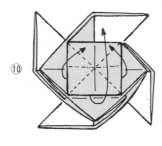

⑩

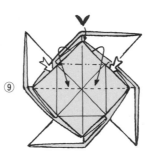

⑨

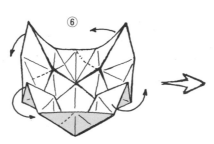

⑧

Employing the creases made to step *4* adjusts the paper into the form shown in step 7.

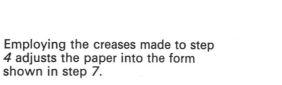

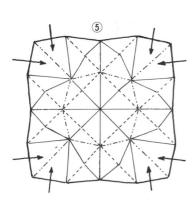

⑤

⑥

⑦

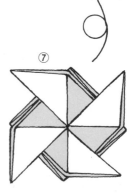

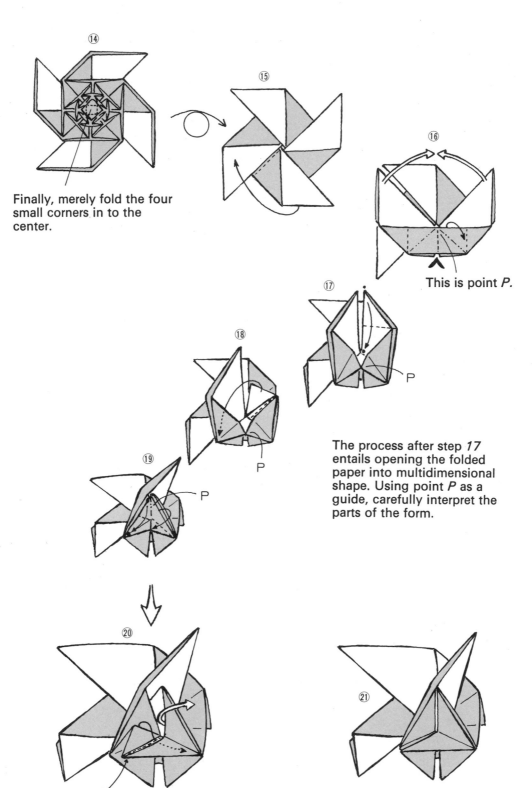

⑭

Finally, merely fold the four small corners in to the center.

⑮

⑯

This is point P.

⑰

P

⑱

P

The process after step 17 entails opening the folded paper into multidimensional shape. Using point P as a guide, carefully interpret the parts of the form.

⑲

P

⑳

P   After opening the pocket on the right and folding the small corner, return the pocket to its former position and push the small corner inward.

㉑

Repeating the process in steps 16–20 in the remaining three parts completes the form.

As in the case of the flower-cut hard-boiled egg, the folder has chosen a strange model. Though the work is entirely different from the real thing, it radiates wonderfully the image of a pine cone.

In this instance, all I received from Mr. Kawasaki was the completed, closed figure and had to puzzle out the folding process. But, once the folding method is learned, this is a very easy origami to produce.

Front side

Back side

Spiral Snail Shell

Toshikazu Kawasaki

Because of its unusual folding method, Mr. Kawasaki's snail shell generates a greater sense of volume than any of the other numerous origami for univalve and bivalve shells. The following three works all involve what could be called the spiral folding technique.

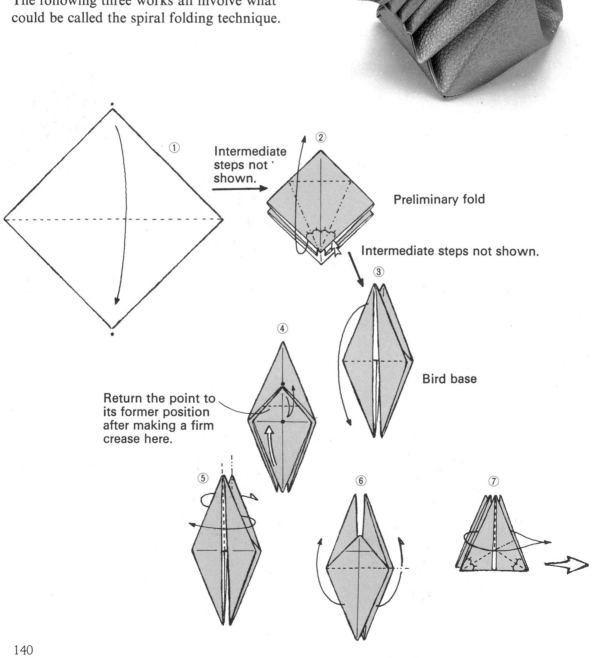

① Intermediate steps not shown.

② Preliminary fold

Intermediate steps not shown.

③ Bird base

④ Return the point to its former position after making a firm crease here.

⑤ ⑥ ⑦

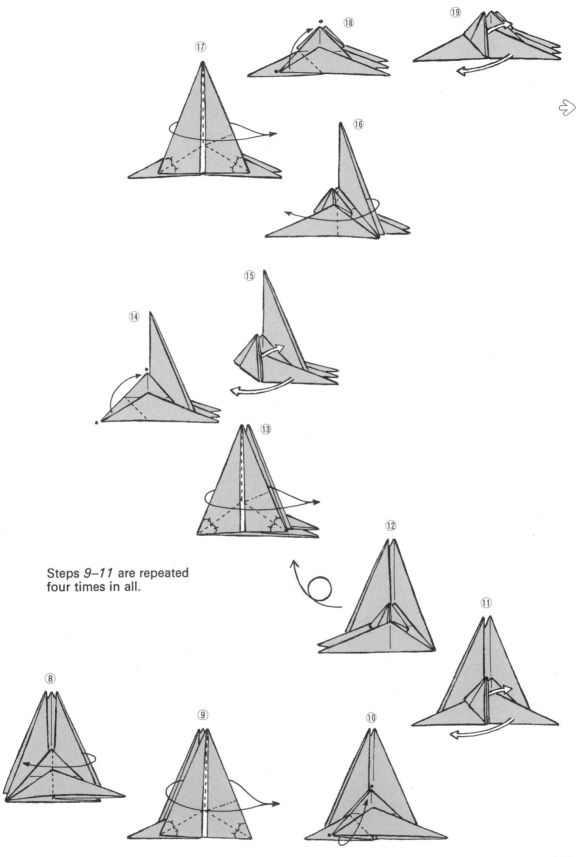

Steps *9–11* are repeated
four times in all.

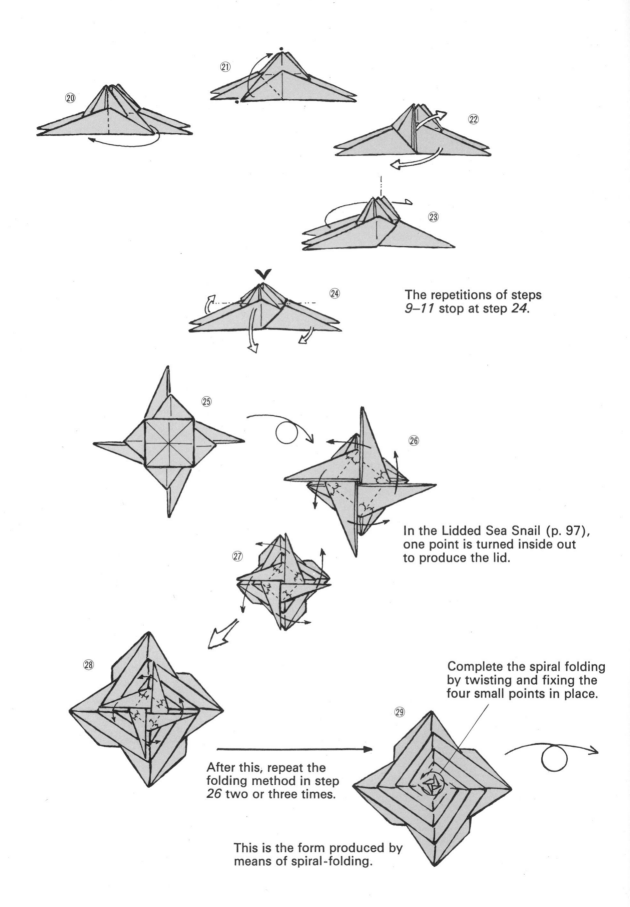

㉑

㉒

㉓

㉔ The repetitions of steps
9–11 stop at step *24*.

㉕

㉖ In the Lidded Sea Snail (p. 97),
one point is turned inside out
to produce the lid.

㉗

㉘

Complete the spiral folding
by twisting and fixing the
four small points in place.

㉙

After this, repeat the
folding method in step
26 two or three times.

This is the form produced by
means of spiral-folding.

The completed shell

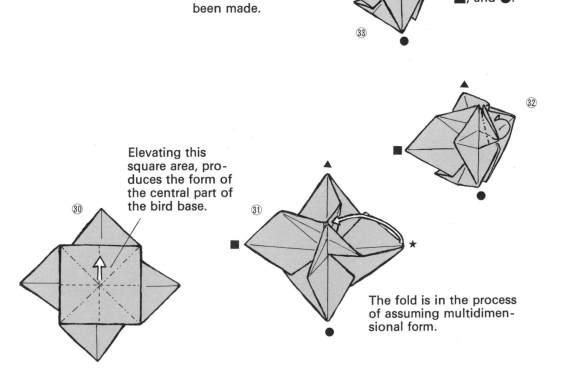

③⑥

③⑤ Pull out the
inner pleats.

The version in the photograph
resulted from divising a way to
reduce the number of holes
from four to one.

Invert
the figure.

③④

All folds have
been made.

▲

■   ●

③③

Now perform the
folding in steps *31*
and *32* on the other
corners marked ▲,
■, and ●.

▲
                                        ■   ③②

Elevating this
square area, pro-
duces the form of
the central part of
the bird base.

③⓪

▲
③①

■   ★

●

●

The fold is in the process
of assuming multidimen-
sional form.

143

Sea-snail Shell

Toshikazu Kawasaki

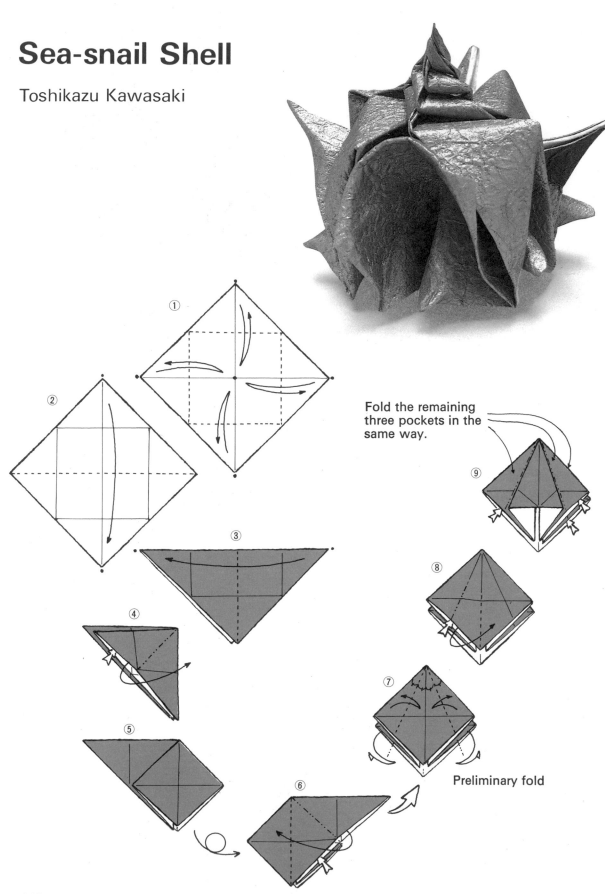

① ②

Fold the remaining
three pockets in the
same way.

⑨

③

④

⑧

⑤

⑦

⑥

Preliminary fold

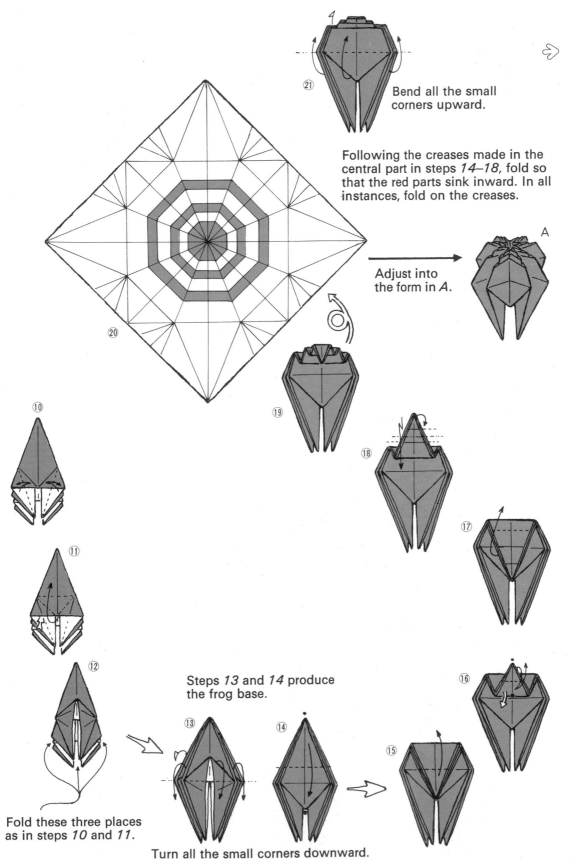

Bend all the small corners upward.

Following the creases made in the central part in steps *14–18*, fold so that the red parts sink inward. In all instances, fold on the creases.

A

Adjust into the form in *A*.

Steps *13* and *14* produce the frog base.

Fold these three places as in steps *10* and *11*.

Turn all the small corners downward.

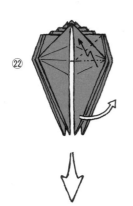

㉒

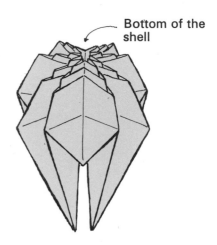

Bottom of the shell

Enlargement of A on the preceding page

It is typical of Mr. Kawasaki's thoroughness to devote attention to making the bottom of the shell, which is not seen when the work is displayed, as lovely as this.

㉓

㉔

As you make the outside reverse fold on the creases produced in step *23*, the double pleats will separate.

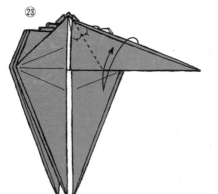

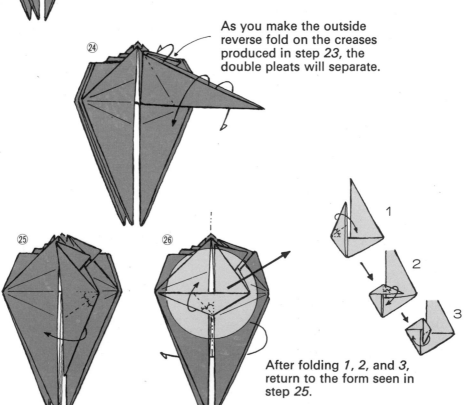

1

2

3

After folding *1, 2,* and *3,* return to the form seen in step *25*.

㉕

㉖

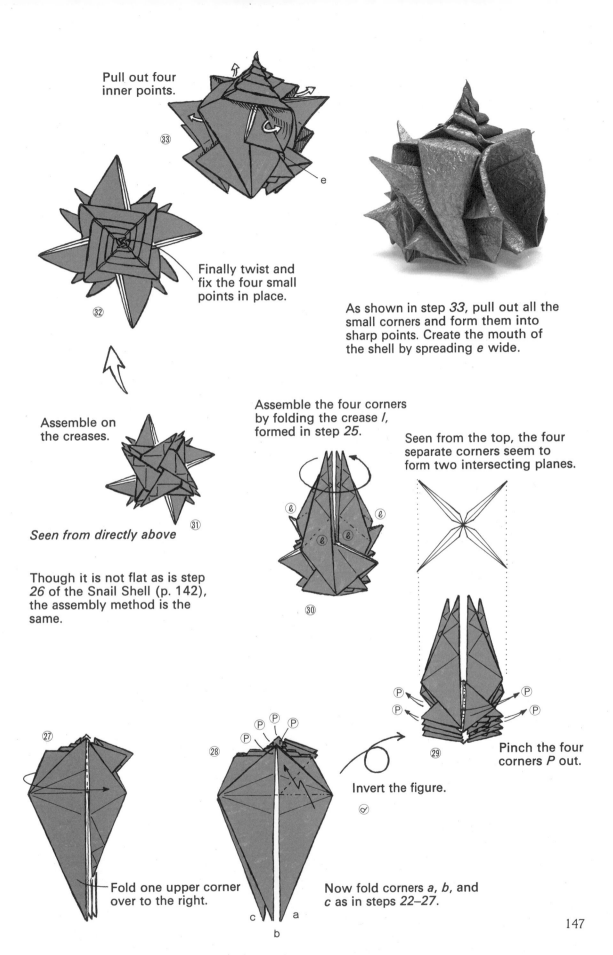

Pull out four
inner points.

㉝

Finally twist and
fix the four small
points in place.

㉜

As shown in step *33*, pull out all the
small corners and form them into
sharp points. Create the mouth of
the shell by spreading *e* wide.

Assemble on
the creases.

Seen from directly above

㉛

Though it is not flat as is step
26 of the Snail Shell (p. 142),
the assembly method is the
same.

Assemble the four corners
by folding the crease *l*,
formed in step *25*.

㉚

Seen from the top, the four
separate corners seem to
form two intersecting planes.

Pinch the four
corners *P* out.

㉙

Invert the figure.

㉗

Now fold corners *a*, *b*, and
c as in steps *22–27*.

㉘

Fold one upper corner
over to the right.

147

Murex Shell

Toshikazu Kawasaki

A minimum of cutting makes it much easier to produce the numerous spines characteristic of the murex shell.

Beginning with the frog base, step *13* of the Sea-snail shell, fold one point over to the left.

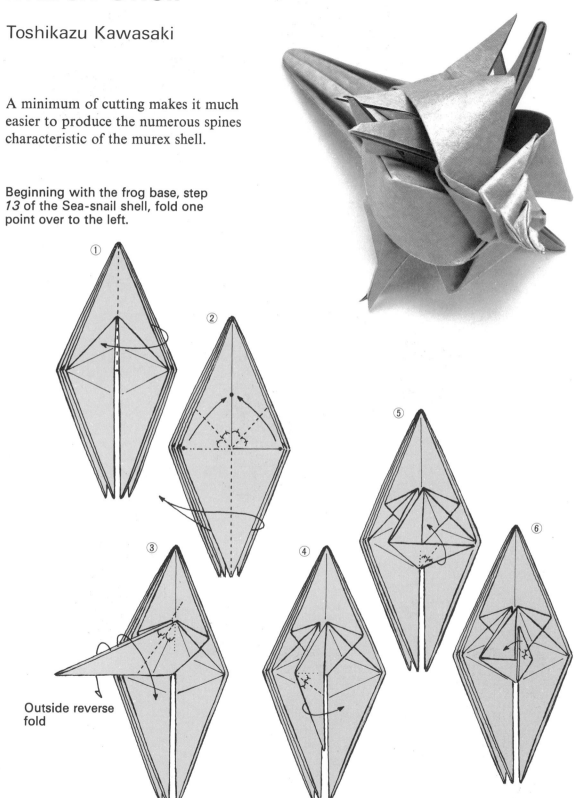

Outside reverse fold

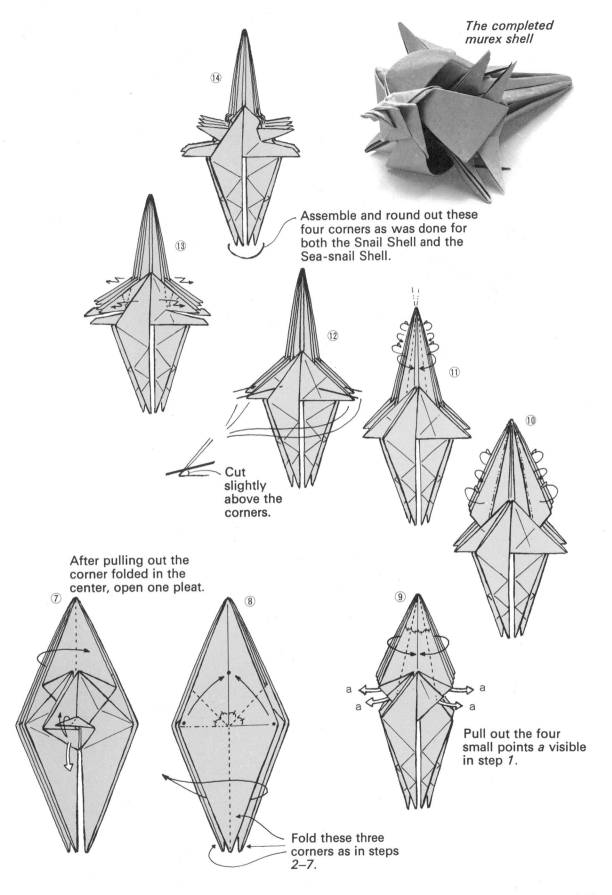

The completed murex shell

⑭

Assemble and round out these four corners as was done for both the Snail Shell and the Sea-snail Shell.

⑬

⑫

⑪

⑩

Cut slightly above the corners.

After pulling out the corner folded in the center, open one pleat.

⑦

⑧

⑨

a   a

a   a

Pull out the four small points *a* visible in step *1*.

Fold these three corners as in steps 2–7.

Ground Beetle

John Montroll

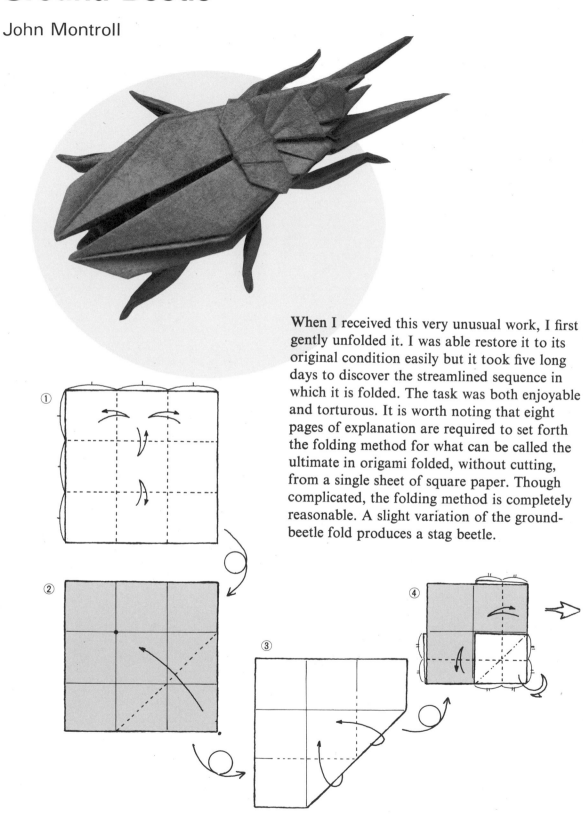

When I received this very unusual work, I first gently unfolded it. I was able restore it to its original condition easily but it took five long days to discover the streamlined sequence in which it is folded. The task was both enjoyable and torturous. It is worth noting that eight pages of explanation are required to set forth the folding method for what can be called the ultimate in origami folded, without cutting, from a single sheet of square paper. Though complicated, the folding method is completely reasonable. A slight variation of the ground-beetle fold produces a stag beetle.

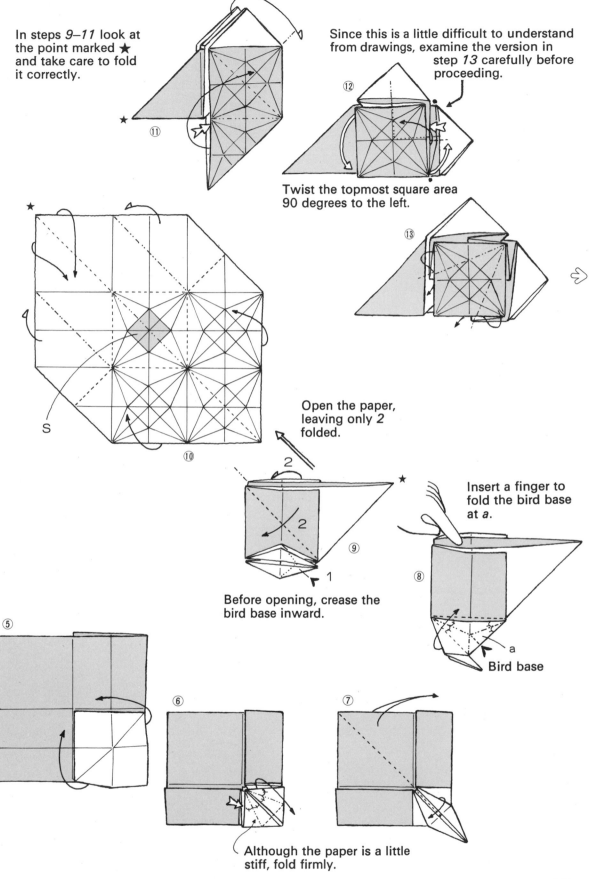

In steps *9–11* look at the point marked ★ and take care to fold it correctly.

⑪

Since this is a little difficult to understand from drawings, examine the version in step *13* carefully before proceeding.

⑫

Twist the topmost square area 90 degrees to the left.

⑬

★

S

⑩

Open the paper, leaving only *2* folded.

2

2

⑨

1

Before opening, crease the bird base inward.

★

Insert a finger to fold the bird base at *a*.

⑧

a

Bird base

⑤

⑥

⑦

Although the paper is a little stiff, fold firmly.

151

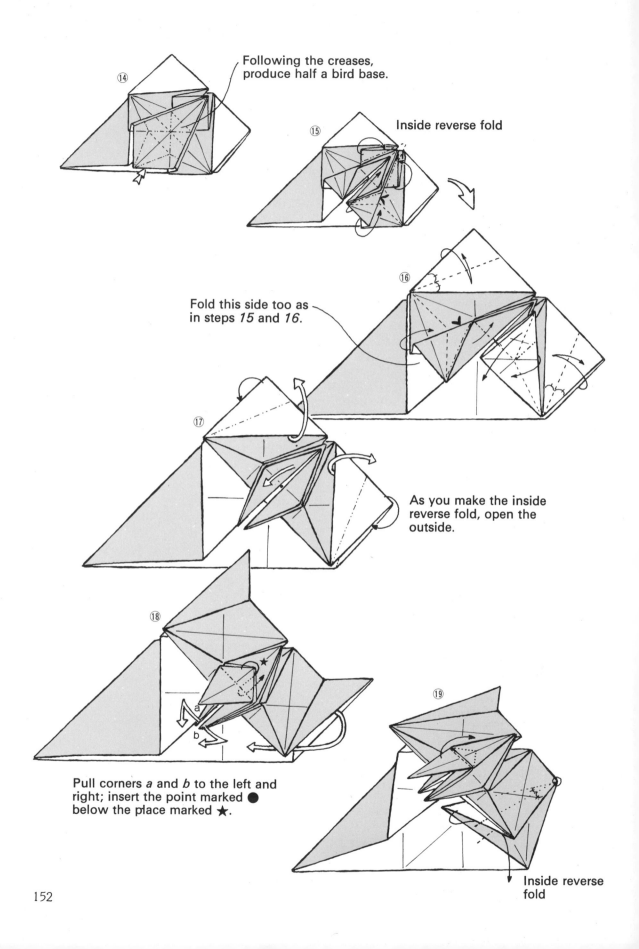

Following the creases,
produce half a bird base.

Inside reverse fold

Fold this side too as
in steps *15* and *16*.

As you make the inside
reverse fold, open the
outside.

Pull corners *a* and *b* to the left and
right; insert the point marked ●
below the place marked ★.

Inside reverse
fold

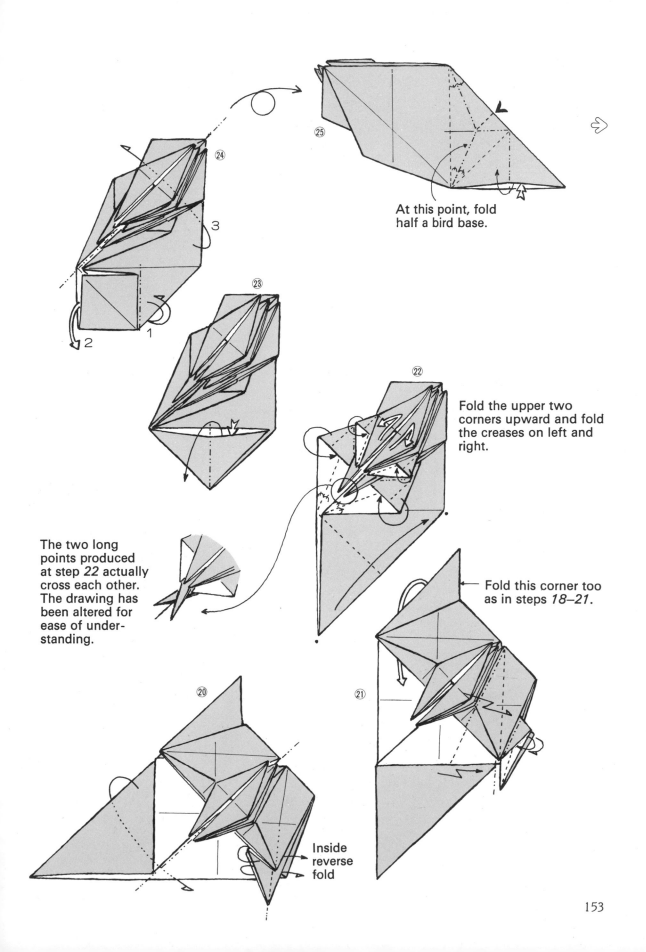

㉕ At this point, fold
half a bird base.

③

② ① 2

㉓

㉒ Fold the upper two
corners upward and fold
the creases on left and
right.

The two long
points produced
at step *22* actually
cross each other.
The drawing has
been altered for
ease of under-
standing.

Fold this corner too
as in steps *18–21*.

㉑

⑳

Inside
reverse
fold

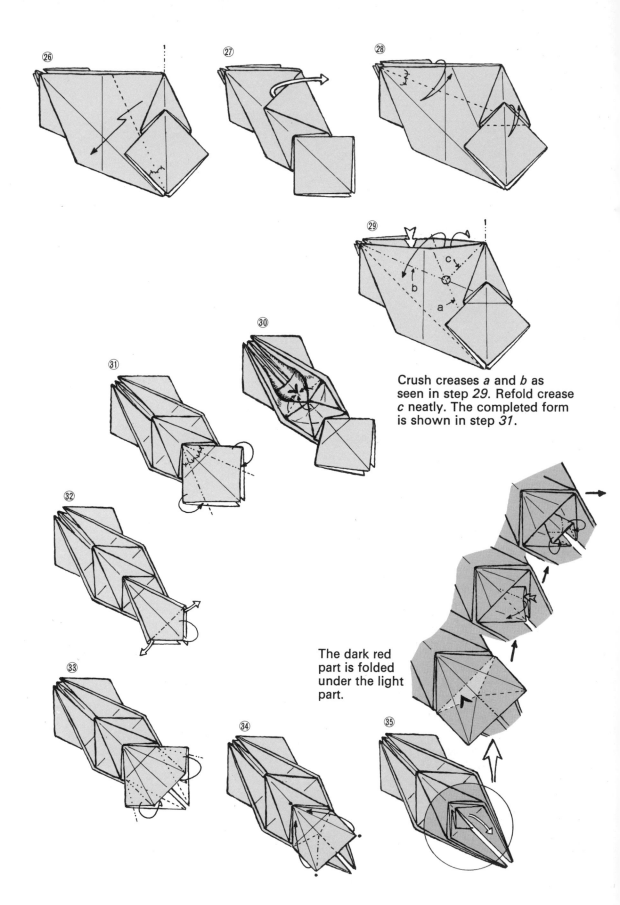

Crush creases *a* and *b* as seen in step *29*. Refold crease *c* neatly. The completed form is shown in step *31*.

The dark red part is folded under the light part.

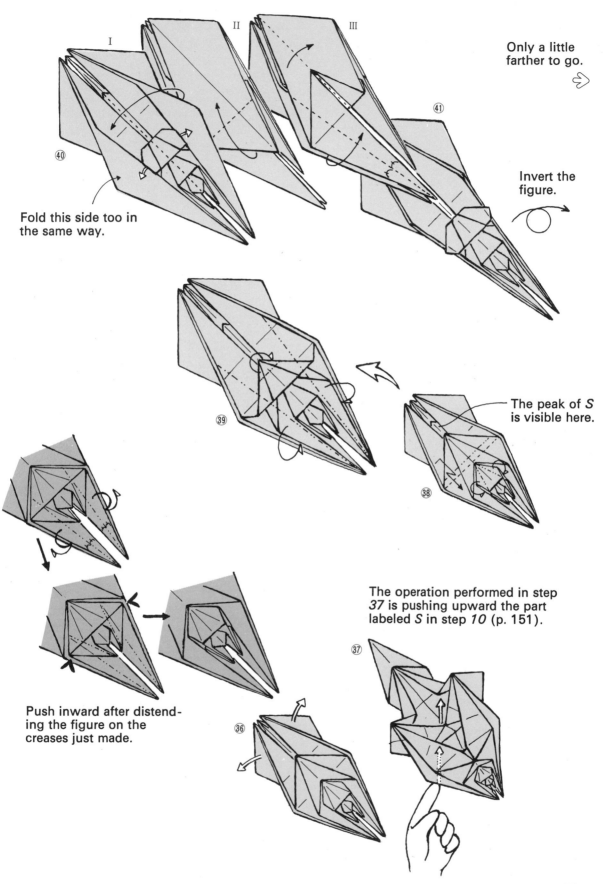

I II III

Only a little
farther to go.

⤵

④

④

Invert the
figure.

Fold this side too in
the same way.

The peak of *S*
is visible here.

③

③

The operation performed in step
37 is pushing upward the part
labeled *S* in step *10* (p. 151).

③

Push inward after distend-
ing the figure on the
creases just made.

③

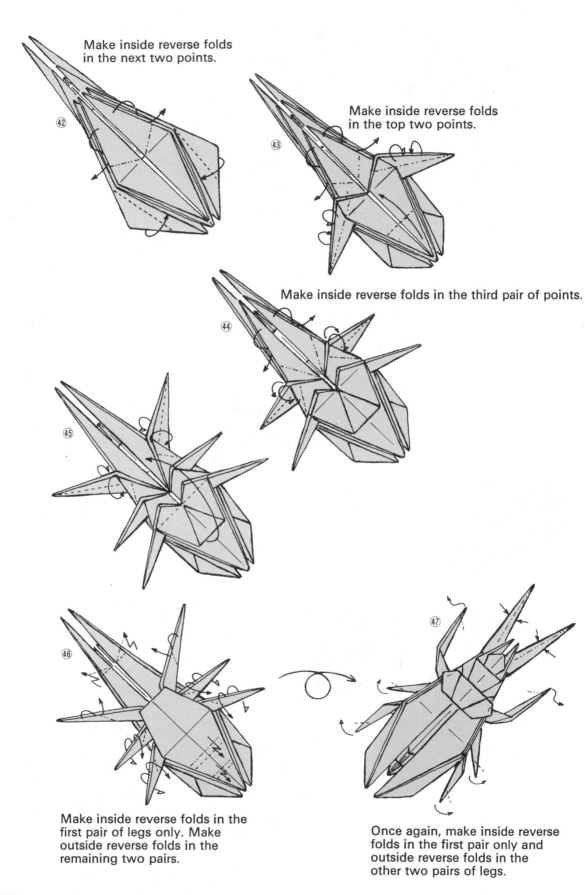

Make inside reverse folds in the next two points.

㊷

Make inside reverse folds in the top two points.

㊸

Make inside reverse folds in the third pair of points.

㊹

㊺

㊻

Make inside reverse folds in the first pair of legs only. Make outside reverse folds in the remaining two pairs.

㊼

Once again, make inside reverse folds in the first pair only and outside reverse folds in the other two pairs of legs.

156

Since the method provides everything needed for three pairs of legs, antennae, mouth, and wings, once you have mastered the folding for the ground beetle, it should be easy to work out variations. One such—a stag beetle—is shown in the photograph.

Stag beetle

Congratulations, you made it!

Completed ground beetle

Ramphorhynchus

John Montroll

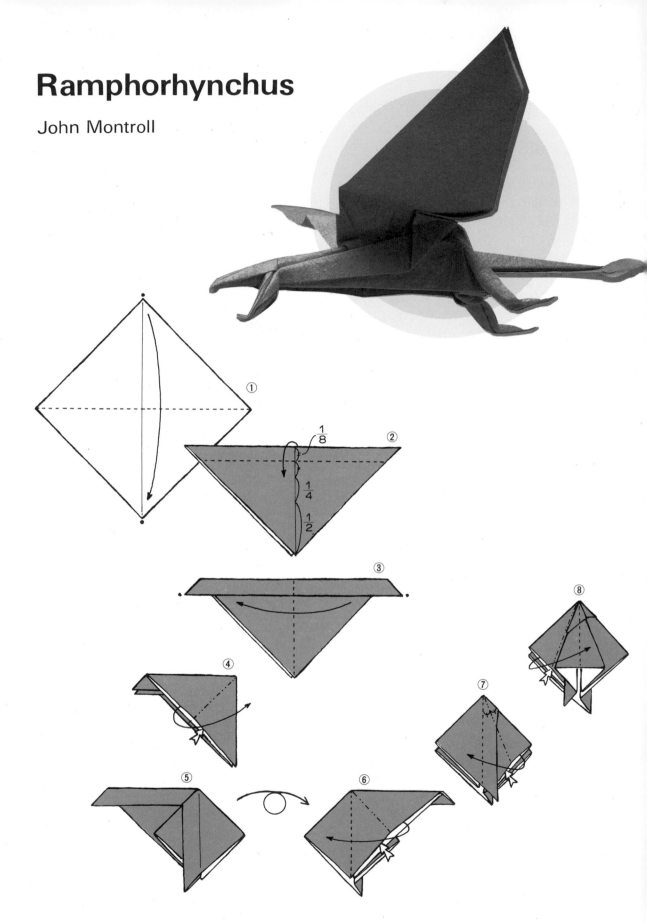

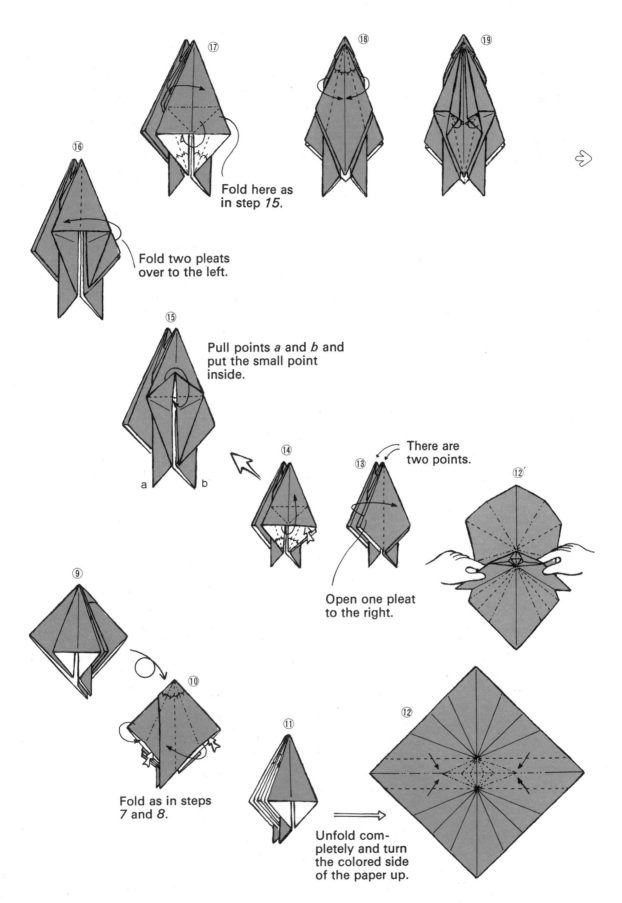

⑰ Fold here as in step *15*.

⑯ Fold two pleats over to the left.

⑮ Pull points *a* and *b* and put the small point inside.

a   b

⑭

There are two points.

⑬

Open one pleat to the right.

⑫´

⑨

⑩ Fold as in steps *7* and *8*.

⑪

Unfold completely and turn the colored side of the paper up.

⑫

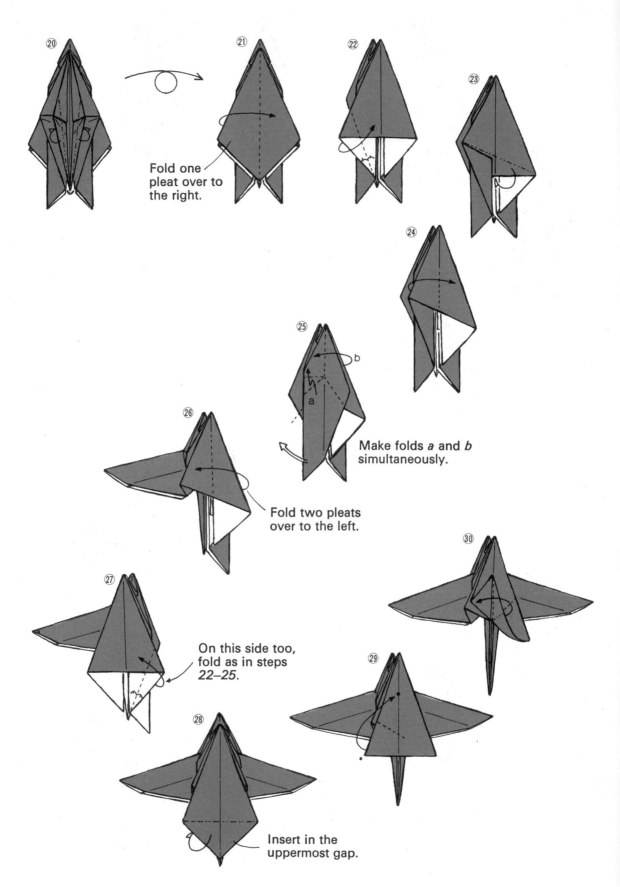

Fold one pleat over to the right.

Make folds *a* and *b* simultaneously.

Fold two pleats over to the left.

On this side too, fold as in steps *22–25*.

Insert in the uppermost gap.

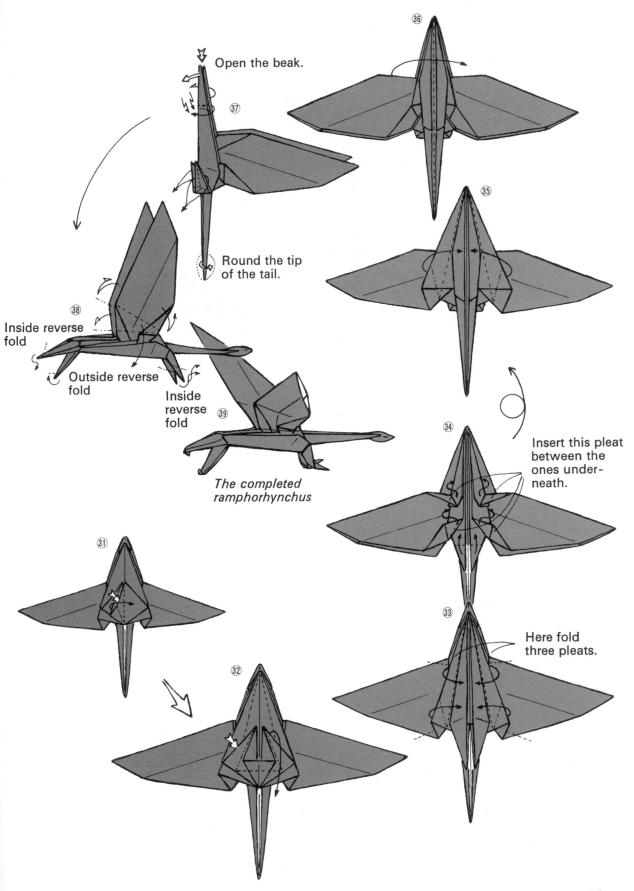

Open the beak.

③⑦

Round the tip
of the tail.

③⑧
Inside reverse
fold

Outside reverse
fold

Inside
reverse
fold

③⑨

*The completed
ramphorhynchus*

③⑥

③⑤

③④
Insert this pleat
between the
ones under-
neath.

③③
Here fold
three pleats.

③①

③②

Stegosaurus

John Montroll

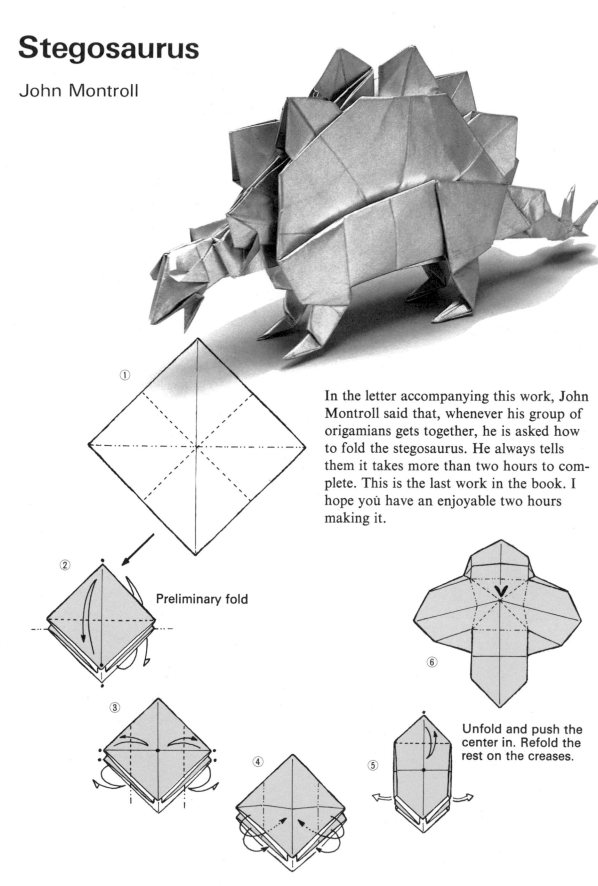

In the letter accompanying this work, John Montroll said that, whenever his group of origamians gets together, he is asked how to fold the stegosaurus. He always tells them it takes more than two hours to complete. This is the last work in the book. I hope you have an enjoyable two hours making it.

①

② Preliminary fold

③

④

⑤

⑥

Unfold and push the center in. Refold the rest on the creases.

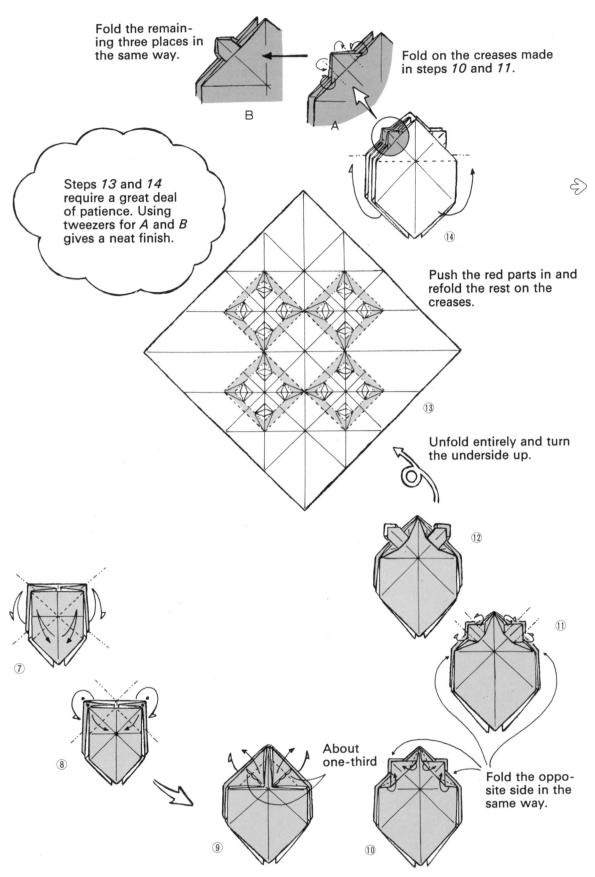

Fold the remaining three places in the same way.

B

Fold on the creases made in steps *10* and *11*.

A

Steps *13* and *14* require a great deal of patience. Using tweezers for *A* and *B* gives a neat finish.

⑭

Push the red parts in and refold the rest on the creases.

⑬

Unfold entirely and turn the underside up.

⑫

⑪

⑦

⑧

About one-third

Fold the opposite side in the same way.

⑨

⑩

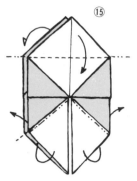

(15)

Both are inside reverse folds.

Mr. Montroll has carefully expressed such details as the staggered arrangement of the finlike plates projecting from the stegosaurus's back—a characteristic that is apparent in graphic renditions of the creature. The processes shown in step *25* indicate how this subtle artistic effect is produced.

After the drawings for this book were completed, Mr. Montroll taught me his way of folding the stegosaurus. His system for folding the legs from step *25* is much more rhythmical than mine. But, since my version successfully produces the fold, I left the drawings unaltered.

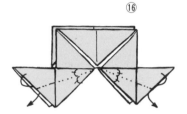

(16)

Both are inside reverse folds.

(17)

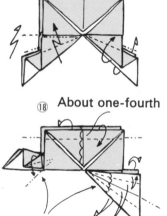

(18) About one-fourth

Fold the opposite side in the same way.

The completed head

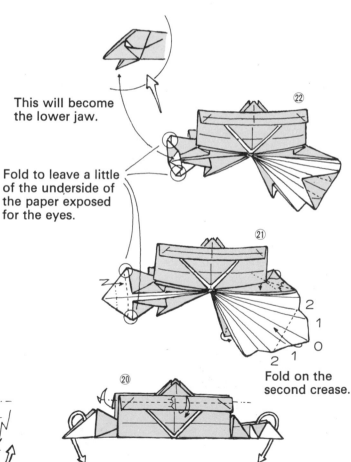

This will become the lower jaw.

Fold to leave a little of the underside of the paper exposed for the eyes.

(22)

(21)

Fold on the second crease.

(19)

(20)

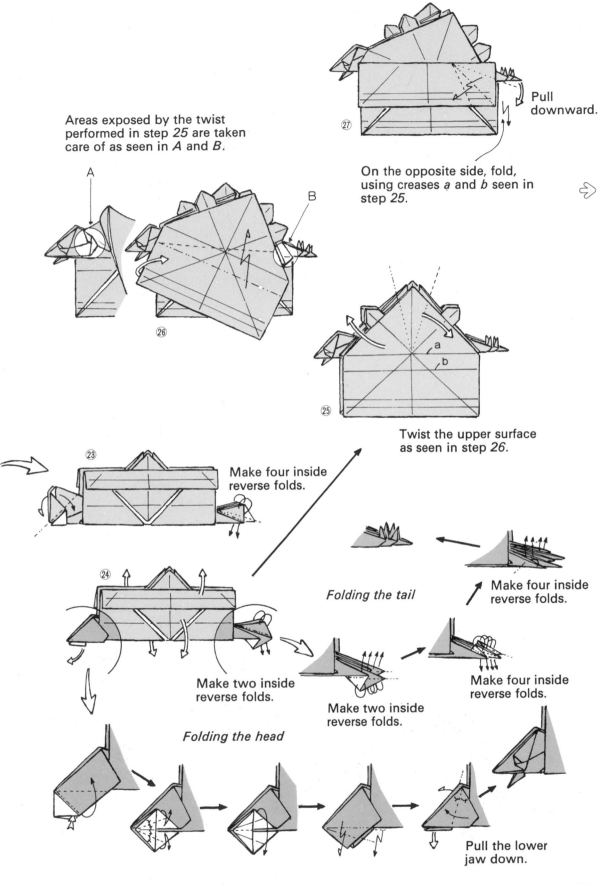

Areas exposed by the twist performed in step *25* are taken care of as seen in *A* and *B*.

A

B

㉖

Pull downward.

On the opposite side, fold, using creases *a* and *b* seen in step *25*.

a
b

㉗

㉕

Twist the upper surface as seen in step *26*.

㉓

Make four inside reverse folds.

㉔

Make two inside reverse folds.

Folding the head

Folding the tail

Make four inside reverse folds.

Make two inside reverse folds.

Make four inside reverse folds.

Pull the lower jaw down.

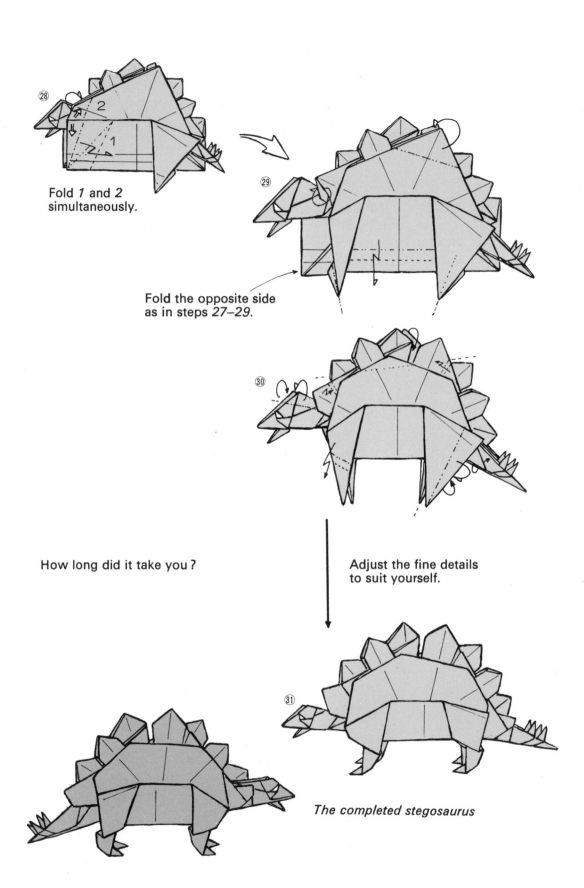

㉘ Fold *1* and *2*
simultaneously.

㉙ Fold the opposite side
as in steps *27–29*.

㉚

How long did it take you?

Adjust the fine details
to suit yourself.

㉛

The completed stegosaurus

Postscript

Japanese atomic physicist Dr. Kohji Fushimi, who participated in the compilation of this book, is only one of the many people today who lament the exclusion of the study called elementary geometry from the curricula of schools in many of the industrialized nations of the world. In this practical age, when numbers take pride of place, a person's abilities are frequently judged solely on the basis of correct or incorrect numerical values entered on test papers.

Geometry cannot be limited in this way. The time that a person spends in deep concentration on the drawing of a single auxiliary line in a geometry problem is filled with reward and pleasure, even though the process may be so absorbing that the final solution of the problem is wrong. I suspect that all readers who have enjoyed the origami masterpieces introduced in this book have, to an extent, tasted the joy experienced by the creators as they used their fingertips to discover various forms. No practical value is to be derived from reproducing David Brill's bottle or the geometric forms of Jun Maekawa and Kazuo Haga. It may have taken two or three hours of hard work to finish Peter Engel's Kangaroo or John Montroll's ground beetle, and the results may have been neat or messy. Nonetheless, if you had a good time doing it, you have shared the feelings experienced by the originators of the folds.

If and when geometry is granted its former place in our system of education, I am convinced that origami can be important material in its instruction. But still more significant, I believe—and am confident the other participants in the production of this book share my belief—that increasing the number of people who take pleasure in origami can help us return to our lives the sense of breadth and ease and the willingness to learn by taking detours and by persisting in the process of trial and error that society is now in danger of losing.